Do things before you're ready.

ITCH

A PACIFIC NORTHWEST TRAIL STORY

1248 MILES IN 4 WEEKS

NICK FOWLER

HERE FOR THE
TAKING

This book is full of bad advice. I don't recommend attempting anything I say or do. I'm the opposite of a medical professional and generally have no idea what I'm talking about. Anything offensive in this book is made up. Everything super cool is true.

Here for the Taking and its colophon are registered trademarks.

Cover art: Dave Cole
Map: Hannah Fowler
Foreword: Jeff Garmire
Hannah's Version: Hannah Fowler
Nick's Mom's Perspective: Nick's Mom
Editor: Stephanie Fields
Design and layout for cover and text: Six Penny Graphics
All photographs by author unless credited otherwise

Publisher's Cataloging-in-Publication data

Names: Fowler, Nick, author.
Title: Itch : a Pacific Northwest Trail story , 1248 miles in 4 weeks / Nick Fowler.
Description: Tulsa, OK: Here for the Taking, 2024.
Identifiers: LCCN: 2023924507 | ISBN: 979-8-9897490-0-3 (paperback) | 979-8-9897490-1-0 (ebook)
Subjects: LCSH Fowler, Nick--Travel--Pacific Northwest Trail. | Walking--Pacific Northwest Trail. | Hiking--Pacific Northwest Trail. | Pacific Northwest Trail--Discovery and exploration. | BISAC TRAVEL / Special Interest / Hikes & Walks | TRAVEL / United States / West / Pacific (AK, CA, HI, OR, WA) | SPORTS & RECREATION / Hiking
Classification: LCC GV199.42.P33 F69 2024 | DDC 917.950444--dc23

Printed in the United States of America

ISBN (print): 979-8-9897490-0-3
ISBN (ebook): 979-8-9897490-1-0

To Hannah -
I couldn't have done it without you.

TABLE OF CONTENTS

THE PACIFIC
NORTHWEST TRAIL

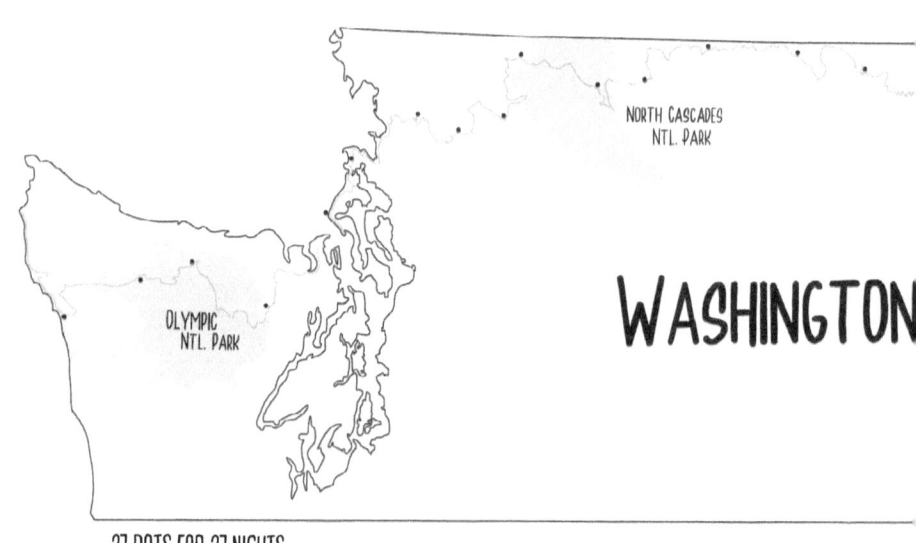

NORTH CASCADES
NTL. PARK

OLYMPIC
NTL. PARK

WASHINGTON

• 27 DOTS FOR 27 NIGHTS

1,248 MILES
7 MOUNTAIN RANGES
3 NATIONAL PARKS

FOREWORD

BY JEFF GARMIRE

A THRU-HIKE IS THE UNDERTAKING of a goal that is so massive that the magnitude of it is impossible to comprehend. And the Pacific Northwest Trail takes thru-hiking to another level. The ruggedness, remoteness, and distance between towns add a difficulty not seen on many other trails. Making it a first thru-hike is bold, to say the least. Making it a first thru-hike AND going after the record on the trail takes it to an entirely new level. Not only does it require flexibility, determination, and toughness, but also the continued drive to move forward no matter what weather, conditions, or adversity is thrown at you.

The Pacific Northwest Trail showcases some of the most remote yet beautiful areas of the country that are also some of the most difficult to reach. Within the first 100 miles, thru-hikers get to traverse the beach, battle the tides, climb the rugged headlands, climb through the rain forests, and venture across the alpine. And the diversity of the trail only continues from there. Crossing two national scenic trails, three national parks, and seven national forests, the PNT is a more epic immersement into nature than any other national scenic trail in the country. It is the perfect setting for a hiker from Oklahoma to morph into an elite athlete.

My first time adventuring with Nick was an early-season adventure in Grand Teton National Park. The high country was covered in snow, and that is exactly why we chose to venture up into it. Our common interest in finding adventure immediately drew us together, and we treated the alpine areas as a playground. Instead of continuing on the snow-covered trails, we went up and down the Paintbrush Divide multiple times and glissaded down. It was the pure joy of adventure that brought us together, the very thing I strive to find in each of my own adventures. It is that same playful theme that shines through Nick's epic adventure on the PNT and makes the fastest time ever on the trail relatable to any reader.

Nick Fowler's decision to take on his first thru-hike at the same time as the Fastest Known Time speaks to a drive far exceeding many people that I have met. But it is not the physical determination that makes the story of setting the record so intriguing, but the continued focus on joy, beauty, and acceptance of the privilege to get to accept such an undertaking. A story that intertwines a great support system, a dream, and the motivation to take the steps to get it done. The love and encouragement coming from home is such an important through line in any adventure, and *Itch* captures it perfectly. It gives me hope and inspiration that such a strong and fundamental bond in a partnership can lead to incredible accomplishments.

The immersement in a goal is what makes this book special. It is something rarely displayed so well with a passion that shines off the page. Even with adversity, gear failure, and discomfort beginning on day one, the problem-solving mindset of a true thru-hiker was present from the get-go. While an FKT is never a sure thing, from the very first page, it is never a question that Nick will enjoy the journey and bring you along for a wonderful ride through the Pacific Northwest. As a trail that few choose to hike each year, simply reading the story of a man chasing passion and a goal will fill you with the inspiration to adventure. *Itch* is the story of a man having a dream, making it a goal, creating a plan, and then putting everything into making it a reality.

FORT DRY BRIDGE

THE PRESSURE DROPS. Thunder rumbles. Dark, ominous rain clouds bleed across the sky. A storm is being summoned.

My pace quickens; I'd really rather get off this mountain before the rain starts again. All I have left are flats and downhills until I get out of Washington. I'll be in Idaho in just a few hours.

A steady drizzle begins. I quickly throw on my rain jacket. As I make my way down off the exposed ridgeline, the vegetation crowding out the trail grows thicker. It's completely soaked. It must have been raining hard here a few minutes ago. It's only a matter of time before it dumps on me. *I need to start running.* Plowing through the overgrowth, I can barely see the trail at my feet—it's hard to run when you can't see where your feet are going to land. I start a slow jog anyway. *At least if I trip over something, I'll be moving slow enough to catch myself.*

The rain gets heavier and heavier as it gets darker and darker. As I continue to go down in elevation, the trail opens up and gets wider. I'm no longer swimming through leaves. *Of course it's not overgrown with wet vegetation. It's a complete downpour. The trail doesn't need wet plants to keep my feet wet anymore.*

The farther down the mountain I go, the bigger the trees get. Eventually, I find myself in an old-growth cedar forest with trunks so big they could swallow a car. They're tall, mysterious, and wise. Untouched and unscathed by man, they're inviting—even in the midst of a storm. *How is this not a national park?* Only it's better. It's national park quality without the crowds. *Yeah, until some douchebag comes along and writes about it.* Too bad it's raining; I'd love to get some pictures to remember this side of the mountain better. The monstrous trees, moss, and huge ferns suggest this forest gets plenty to drink—it probably rains here all the time.

Crack—Kaboom!!

The storm continues to grow in power. The trail lights up bright with the next lightning flash. I count, "One one thou…"

Boom!

The thunder doesn't even take a full second after the lightning. The center of the storm is getting closer.

Flash!

The trail lights up again followed by more explosive thunder. The bright flash reveals a cluster of blown-down trees across the trail up ahead. *Surely it's just this patch of trees. The trail has been fairly clear of blowdowns for several days… or maybe that means it's overdue…* I crawl through the maze of deadfall and get back on trail. I turn the corner, and my headlamp shows the next batch of collapsed trees. *I guess it was overdue.*

A few miles later, lightning cracks all around with no delay in the thunder. The wind roars. *Phaboom.* I hear trees falling in the woods not too far away. The trail is two inches deep in rainwater and mud. I lift my right leg up on a slightly angled, blown-down tree to climb up and over it. As I lift my left leg off the ground, my right foot slips on the wet bark, and I fall forward across the toppled mess. My side lands on the sharp end of a broken-off tree limb as I fall to the other side. How that tree limb didn't impale my skin is a mystery. My left leg is bleeding again, though. "Surprise, surprise," I mumble as I stand up and wipe mud off my face, shoulder, and legs. *But hey—at least I'm not a shish kabob.*

A couple of hours later, I arrive at another trail junction; it's still storming. The trail junctions out here are not marked for the Pacific Northwest Trail (PNT), so I'm constantly having to check my GPS location against the map to verify I'm headed in the right direction. Sometimes there are more trail junctions in person than are indicated on my map. That, and I can somehow magically miss certain details when I'm exhausted at the end of a long day. OK, it might mainly just be me. Either way, GPS is flat-out handy—I've missed too many turns and wasted too much time not to keep a close eye on it.

The towel I've been using to wipe my phone screen dry is now sopping wet. Have you ever tried to use a phone screen when it's wet? They just don't work. I search for any potential spot under a tree that might be dry. If I can just get out from under the rain, I might be able to figure out where I'm at. I navigate off-trail under the biggest trees I can find and fiddle with my phone. Rain still finds its way through somehow. I frantically wipe the screen, hoping that fast friction will somehow dry it off. It actually works—once. I can operate my map for a couple of seconds. Enough to figure out my next turn. Keep moving.

Eventually I make it to the trailhead, which means I'm back on dirt forest service roads until I get back on another foot trail. My so-called "waterproof" rain jacket has soaked through. Everything is saturated. It's pitch black out and getting cold, fast. I come to a fork in the road. I'm not sure which way to go; there are no signs. My fast-friction phone screen dry-out trick isn't working. I pull out my paper map, but it's floppy, wet, and falling apart. It shreds as it comes out of my pocket. No potential dry spots are anywhere in sight. I can't just stay here; I need to keep moving to stay warm. I'm not really sure which way to go, but it *feels* like Upper Priest Lake is to the right—I go right.

I'm exhausted, soaking wet, cold, depleted, and emotional. I'm on the brink of crying and just praying for a miracle. *Something's got to give; please just give me something.* I don't know where I am. I could be going in the right direction. I could be going in the wrong direction.

Something has got to give.

Within minutes, I find a bridge. *I can get out from under the rain, dry a couple of pieces of gear off, and at least figure out where I'm at—if I'm on trail or if I'm headed in the wrong direction.* As I'm approaching, I see a flat spot underneath it. *It's going to be freezing soon. I could sleep dry and warm RIGHT there.* But I have to figure out where I am first.

I try to wipe my phone screen off, but all I do is smear water across it. I empty my backpack and lay everything out on the concrete underneath the bridge, hoping it'll dry off while knowing it's not really going to dry off in these dark, wet conditions anyway. Only three items are not completely soaked, a pair of socks and my backpacking quilt—but it's more than enough to return my phone screen to operational status. *Boom, back in business.* I open up Guthooks, the map app I've been primarily using to navigate the trail, step to the side of the bridge for a GPS signal, and voila! I'm headed in the right direction. But... I'm still nine miles away from where I wanted to get to for the night. I have two options. A) Memorize the turns and distance between the turns to make sure I can make the next nine miles, or B) Take this bridge as my miracle and sleep here tonight.

I opt for the miracle.

Welcome to Fort Dry Bridge, my new home for the night.

THE ITCH

I'VE NEVER SET AN FKT (Fastest Known Time) before. Heck, I didn't even know what an FKT was nine months ago. But eight months ago, that's when I knew I wanted one.

Three years ago, my wife Hannah and I left on a year-long road trip to see every national park as a ten-year anniversary present to each other. We liked it so much, it evolved into nearly three years of full-time traveling before we decided to settle back down. You might be envisioning us flying around the country in first class, moving from one resort to the next, staying in lodges, and taking all the guided park tours. In reality, we were camping and living in our van—sometimes even down by a river. When we first started hiking, I remember huffing and puffing after just two miles. That grew to four miles. Four grew to six. When we finally did a whole eight miles in Rocky Mountain National Park, it felt like it took all day, and we were pretty wiped out afterward.

After months of rushing around, seeing national parks in two to three-day stints, we slowed down. We intended to stay in the Redwoods for a week. We ended up staying three. We intended to stay in Olympic National Park for just a handful of days. We ended up staying nearly a month. Glacier National Park was supposed to be two weeks. It became five.

We wandered so slowly, we missed our window to cross into Canada and explore Alaska for the summer. But we were OK with it. We weren't just trying to check every national park off a list anymore. We were enjoying the moment. Soaking in everything that we could. If we liked a place, we'd stay till we were ready to move on. If we weren't super impressed with a place, we'd often move on before the day was over. (It's kind of hard to go from living in the Tetons for three weeks to Theodore Roosevelt National Park in the flatlands of North Dakota.)

In Glacier, a year after we started traveling, we were finally up to regular 10–14 mile day hikes. We were just beginning to get our feet wet with how much beauty you can experience in a 10-plus-mile day. Moose. Iceberg-covered lakes. Cloud-covered tunnels through mountain peaks.

But I wanted to touch a glacier. I didn't want to just see them from a distance. I wanted to touch one with my bare hands. After all, we were in Glacier National Park, I should be able to touch a glacier.

I found out about two side hikes that take you to touch two different glaciers off of Gunsight Pass, an 18.9-mile one-way trail. *Two glaciers in one day? That's a big, fat yes.* I studied the maps (before I even knew how to properly study maps). I couldn't figure out how far these side hikes were to touch the Jackson and Sperry Glaciers. I eventually guesstimated that I'd be adding on two or so miles for each one. By my calculation, it would be 22–24 miles total. *That's a lot of miles. Nearly 10 more than I've ever done in a day, but it's to touch two different glaciers. It'll be worth it.*

Hannah dropped me off on one end around 6:00 a.m.; she'd pick me up on the other before dinner. She had no interest in hiking more than 20 miles. It was the earliest in the morning I'd ever started hiking before. We'd been on "vacation." We'd been sleeping in and taking our time. Moseying around, nonchalantly getting moving whenever we felt like it. But for this hike, to make it back before dark, I needed to start before sunrise.

Within an hour, I came across a couple of moose on the trail. When I looked up, they stood right in front of me, not even 20 feet away—monstrous beasts with a deceptive peace to them. Their muscles shimmered as they exhaled a visible steam through their wide-set nostrils. We made eye contact and paused. No fear was on either part, only mutual respect. Like gentle giants they eventually left the trail to let me pass, walking over shrubs as tall as my shoulders as if it were nothing. *These early morning hikes are where it's at!*

When I arrived at the junction for the Jackson Glacier, I read a sign indicating the overlook was 1.9 miles away. *That's almost four miles round trip just to see it—not even touch it!* Much farther than I was expecting.

I scrambled up the slick limestone moraine channel to the glacier face, navigating the glacial streams that poured out of it. I had never seen a chunk of ice so big before in my life. I placed my hand on it and tilted my head back to gaze straight up the side. It was vibrant. Fresh, yet ancient. Alive. A 40-foot-tall wall of ice, acting as a portal, connecting the past to present. I had never experienced anything quite like that before.

Marmots, mountain goats, and bighorn sheep—the next several hours were pretty social despite me being the only person out there. I was far enough back in the wilderness that I had the entire trail to myself, was having dozens of wildlife encounters, and felt like I was seeing the world for how it was supposed to be before we humans messed it up. One of the mountain goats even followed me for close to a mile. It was special. It was energizing. It was a hook, and the mountains were reeling me in.

Eventually, I found myself at the junction for the side hike off to the Sperry Glacier. My legs were tired, but the mountains were feeding me with energy. The sign read, "Sperry Glacier, 3.7 miles." *It's 7.4 more miles roundtrip!? Oh well. I came out here to touch some glaciers. Let's do this!*

Switchback after switchback I climbed. I kept going up and over rocky moraine fields, expecting to see the glacier at any moment. *This is the moraine; the glacier should be next.* But the fields of boulders and talus just kept going and going. No one told me this glacier was practically on top of a mountain. *That's because you didn't ask anyone, Nick. You just glanced at a map that you didn't even know how to read.*

Eventually I made it. I touched the glacier, took a picture, turned around, and went back. I wasn't nearly as excited to touch it as I was the first glacier, though. The sun was going down. Hannah would be arriving to pick me up at the parking lot soon, and I was still on top of this mountain.

My stomach rumbled as I plodded down the trail. I rummaged through my bag for my last snack, knowing it was already gone but hoping for a crumb. When I reached for my last water bottle, I felt it crumple with weightlessness. This was before I even knew about water filters. I had been carrying all my water with me from car to car on all my hikes. I refilled a bottle from a stream of crisp, clear glacier melt and got back to moving. From alpine to forest to meadows with moss, the trail seemed to drag on forever.

After the sun went down, I finally made it to the trailhead, but I couldn't find Hannah. *Where is she? Am I too late? Did she go somewhere else to look for me?* I slugged through the parking lot back and forth until I heard the distinct sound of our old Volkswagen Vanagon. I followed the sound, and about a minute later she came around the corner.

My tired crankiness turned into a relieved smile. She was saving me. We drove the 45 minutes out of Glacier National Park and back to our campsite on the Hungry Horse Reservoir. Unfortunately, my legs had cooled down. I could barely move. It took me 10 minutes to shuffle from the van to our campsite, 20 feet away. The hike ended up being 32 miles. I went from hiking 14 miles max in a day, to 32 overnight. I had tricked myself into my first 32-mile day hike.

The next day, I couldn't walk.

But the day after that, I was thinking, "*That was awesome!!*"

And that, my friends, was the beginning of my journey. That was the day I fell in love with trekking high-mileage days through the wilderness. You can see so much, experience so much in a day of hiking this way. The varying views from one mountain to the next, the changing climates, the personalities that shift from forest to forest, the flowers, the wildlife, the lakes, and the streams—all just in a 24-hour period. It allows you to go deep enough into the wilderness that you get to see it come alive. And after all, if you're hiking three times as many miles as the average person, you're three times more likely to see a big animal because you're covering more ground, right? I was hooked.

I started seeking out 30-plus-mile day hikes on a regular basis, all with my $20 Walmart backpack and $50 off-brand sneakers that were falling apart. Thirty-six miles through the Timpanogos Wilderness with five summits in a day. Forty-two miles on the Teton Crest Trail without sleeping. Rim to Rim to Rim in the Grand Canyon in less than 24 hours, or so I tried…

The first time I attempted hiking from the South Rim of the Grand Canyon to the North Rim and back to the South, I nearly died.

That day started with me forgetting my ibuprofen in the car at 3:30 a.m. Three miles later, I realized I had forgotten my sandwiches in the cooler, but I wasn't going back three miles to add six miles round trip to the hike. By mile seven, I was squirting diarrhea all over the canyon. *Was it the smoothie I had for breakfast?* It was as if the universe was telling me not to go, but I was too stubborn to listen. My mind was set. *I'm crossing this canyon twice, and I'm doing it today.*

By the time I made it all the way across the canyon and was on my way back down from the North Rim, my body grew weak. Fatigued and woozy, I pressed on. Around four in the afternoon, as I trudged back through The Box, a part of the canyon that traps heat like an oven, my stomach began to turn. I stumbled forward, leaning on gravity to get me to the Colorado River. But as soon as I had to fight the gravity, as soon as I crossed the bridge and started the nine-mile ascent to get out of the canyon, vomit took me to my knees. *Is it the heat? Is this because of the heatstroke I had a few years ago?* Doctors advised heat would be a problem for me, but I never believed them until now. *I'll just take it easy from here. I won't push it; I'll just take my time getting out of here.*

Within half a mile, I was throwing up uncontrollably. I couldn't hold down fluids. If I put even one sip of water in my stomach, I'd throw up more than I had put in within five minutes.

A couple walked past me as I sat on a rock beside the trail. They stopped, turned around, and asked, "Are you OK?"

"No. No, I'm not."

They tended to me for a few minutes. They gave me electrolytes to mix in my water, but unfortunately I couldn't keep anything down at this point. I leaned over the side of the trail, puking and clenching my stomach. Ten minutes went by. I sat in weakness and wiped my face. One of them looked at their watch and whispered to the other.

"Don't worry about me. I'll be fine. You guys go on ahead."

An hour later, the sun dropped behind the canyon walls. I staggered around a corner near a rest house and saw a couple of hikers rummaging through their bags for their headlamps. I sat down on a rock, woozy and dizzy. I attempted a few more swigs; every cell in my body was screaming for water. They asked if I was OK—I started throwing up.

They asked if they could pray over me.

"Of course. Please. I need it."

Halfway through the prayer, I started puking again. I was half lying in the dirt trail, puking uncontrollably, while half trying to keep my body out of the pool of vomit on the ground. *Wait… was that blood?* I thought I saw a dark, thick fluid come out of my mouth on that last heave. I grabbed my headlamp and shined it on the ground for a better look, but everything had already soaked into the sand.

Eventually I got back on my feet and continued moving. I didn't want to hold up these hikers either. It was getting late—late for getting out of the canyon based on where we were. They needed to get back to their car or campsite themselves.

I stumbled forward, 100 feet at a time. I'd stop to sit on a rock, then stand back up and walk a hundred more feet. Stop to take a break on the side of the trail. Repeat.

Another couple of hikers came up behind me, strangers, but we recognized each other. Our paths had crossed that morning. We were all hiking Rim to Rim to Rim in a day. The girl asked, "You alright?" She attempted to encourage me, stating that I was her inspiration to keep going when I passed her earlier.

"No. I can't stop throwing up. I'm so thirsty."

I took another sip of water, then started to heave. Soon there was nothing but bile coming out of my stomach. Everything else had already come up.

The guy, Jonathan, gave me a salt tablet. I swallowed it with a gulp of water, but within minutes the clear liquid was spewing. That salt tablet didn't stand a chance.

Jonathan stressed he was going to stay with me until he knew I was safe. He grabbed my bag, so I didn't have to carry any weight. It helped, but I was still stumbling across the trail, kicking rocks, and swaying back and forth. There were still seven miles to go till the top of the canyon, all steep, and I couldn't even walk straight.

Thirty minutes passed, and I needed another break. We had barely made it a quarter-mile. I lay down in the trail, curled up in the fetal position. Jonathan asserted, "OK, you're not going to make it out of the canyon at this rate. I'm going to go find a ranger for help. Stay lying down in the middle of the trail like this, so if anyone else comes up behind you, they'll see you."

Before they left, Cameron, another hiker, caught up with us. We had all seen each other at some point earlier; we were all hiking with the same mission: Rim to Rim to Rim in a day. I kept lying down on the ground while Jonathan explained the dilemma to Cameron.

"Wait... My sister has a horse!" Cameron shouted, "She was originally planning on camping at the bottom, at Phantom Ranch, but she made a sudden change of mind to come up Bright Angel tonight. She's not too far behind me. I'll go get her."

What seemed like an hour must have only been fifteen minutes. I was too fatigued to gauge an accurate amount of time passing. But eventually, Cameron and Tina showed up with her horse, Jewel, my favorite animal on the planet at this point in my life. Jonathan, Cameron, and Tina all discussed plans on what to do. Tina didn't think she could make it seven more miles out of the canyon hiking; she had planned on riding the horse. Since there was a ranger station at Indian Garden two miles ahead, they decided it would be best to leave me in the ranger's care, supposing and hoping there actually was a ranger there.

I struggled to get on, so they helped me climb up a boulder. Even at saddle height, I strained to swing my leg across the horse's body. My legs cramped up as soon as I sat down. I had to stand up in the stirrups just to keep my legs from screaming. Cameron led Jewel as I attempted leaning on her neck for some relief, but it was to no avail. I had to get off the horse multiple times to throw up in the two-mile stint to get to the ranger station.

By 10:00 p.m., we reached the outpost. I dismounted and sat on the ground while Cameron knocked on the door and explained everything to the ranger, Shane. Shane helped me over to their single clinic bed.

"Can you just stick an IV in me? I can't keep fluids down."

"I'm not a medic. I can't do that. Sorry."

Shane checked my vitals and tried to give me water in extremely small portions to prevent me from throwing up again. He asked me, "Do you have any history or medical conditions I should know about?"

"I had a heat stroke a few years ago that keeps coming back to bite me in the butt. Heat just destroys me now."

I took tiny tastes of the water, swishing it around in my mouth, nervous to swallow. My stomach turned. He gave me some nausea medicine. Five minutes later it was all in a bedpan, including a small amount of blood. Shane called the nurse at the top of the Grand Canyon to consult. They determined since it was such a small amount of blood and super bright red, it was likely just a tear in my throat from too much dry heaving.

He asked me dozens more questions and analyzed the situation: "How much water have you had to drink? What have you eaten? When did you last pee?" He then told me he didn't think I was dehydrated; he thought I had hyponatremia—extremely low sodium. I had plenty of water throughout the day, had salt all over my face from sweat, didn't have much salty food, and was craving a Gatorade and Dr Pepper—both of which have sodium. My body was so diluted, it was refusing to take in any more water until I got more salt in my system. *I shouldn't have swallowed that salt tablet with a gulp of water earlier.*

Shane tore open a chicken ramen noodle seasoning packet and mixed it with 50 mL of water. It was a thick, brothy concoction. I sipped on it over the next 45 minutes. I finished about three-quarters of it and started to feel nauseous, so I stopped. After another 30 minutes, the nausea passed, and my thirst for water kicked in at an entirely different level. I slowly started taking bigger sips, still being cautious because I didn't want to throw up again.

Eventually, I fell asleep, but it didn't last. Cramps jolted me awake throughout the night. They became an internal alarm, reminding me to hydrate. Each time I woke, I drank more water.

When the sun came back up, Shane brought me some words of encouragement along with the best-tasting bowl of salty chili I've ever had in my life, "I hope this bad experience doesn't deter you from hiking big miles." I chowed down, laced up my shoes, and hiked the remaining five miles out of the canyon—with empty spirits.

All that because of salt.

Fast forward to the fall of 2020—I had set a goal to hike over 1,000 miles for the year. I ended up surpassing that 1,000-mile mark as I attempted Rim to Rim to Rim in a day again. This time I crushed it! From one side of the canyon to the other and back, plus 10 extra miles of side hikes and exploring, all in about 18 hours.

The next month, in November, I went back to one of my favorite spots—Buckskin Gulch and the Paria River—the longest and deepest slot canyon in the world. I wanted to find out how far I could go. *I'll just go in as far as I can until I get tired, and then turn around to come back.*

I made it 73 miles that day—by falling on my face. It was mostly easy terrain through an inspiring canyon, but instead of steep climbs, there was soft clay. Muck that was muck on the ground, but muck that became concrete within minutes of attaching to your legs. I can't even tell you how many times I fell in that mud. It wasn't nearly as tough as the Grand Canyon, but it was 73 miles in a day, just for fun nevertheless. I remember stopping to stretch my legs and uttering, "Only 14 more miles to go." *Ha! Who says, "Only 14 more miles to go"?*

That's when I started thinking about thru-hikes: end-to-end back-packing trips long enough that you have to resupply along the way. I had mostly been doing high-mileage day hikes at this point. Any backpacking I had done was usually around 30 miles a day, for no more than a week at a time.

I developed this itch. I started wondering, "What's the fastest anyone's ever hiked the Pacific Crest Trail (PCT)?" I had heard of the PCT before, but when we came across it in North Cascades National Park, I realized how beautiful it was—it had the kind of views that inspire me to hike big miles.

I looked up the records and discovered this website called FastestKnownTime.com (FKT). They split up the records into three styles: supported, self-supported, and unsupported.

Supported means you can have all the help you can dream of as long as you're entirely self-powered. You can have someone preparing your food, carrying your gear, and setting up your tent. You can have someone massaging your feet every night and someone driving into town for more supplies. You can even have pacers running down the trail beside you carrying your water. The beauty in this style is that it allows for pure speed. It's fascinating what people can accomplish with a team.

Self-supported means just that—you're supporting yourself. You can purchase more supplies, pick up resupply boxes, and even beg for help—but you're carrying your own gear and you're out there on your own. It's true thru-hiker style, the way I want to do it.

Unsupported is the hardest; the only thing you can replenish is water from natural sources along the trail. If you're one of the ones that goes after the unsupported category, you're strong as hell, because that bag has to weigh a ton.

I found the PCT FKT page. Heather Anderson held the self-supported record. I did the math: 2,650 miles in 60 days. She averaged 44 miles a day on the PCT—across the country, Mexico to Canada, in less than two months by foot. *Wow, what a hiker.* I had never done that kind of mileage back-to-back, but I thought if I trained for it—maybe I could actually pull it off.

DO MORE THAN KAREL DID

THE MORE I LEARNED about these records, the more it became clear that it's not really possible to beat them by just hiking anymore. You have to implement running. You have to cover enough mileage during the day to give yourself time to recover at night.

I had no clue where to start. I read an interview with the current supported PCT FKT record holder, Karel Sabbe. He did strength training on Mondays and Tuesdays, then ran a marathon before work Wednesday through Friday, and ran another 26–40 miles a day on the weekends. *If that's what Karel did, I need to be able to do more than that.*

And thus I had my training plan: Do more than Karel did.

But as it turned out, I didn't know what I was talking about. I later found out this was not his training plan at all. I either made the whole article up or I was losing my mind. Or maybe... just maybe... the internet was wrong. *Gasp.*

But a marathon a day before work was what I thought his training was at the time. And that's what I acted on. So the story continues.

I hadn't run since high school soccer, 15 years ago. So I needed to build up to what Karel was doing. I started running a half-marathon a day in January. One day, an armadillo ran out from under a pile of leaves next to the trail as I was in the air, mid-stride. It ran under my foot as I was landing. It was like trying to run on a bowling ball. I went down. The armadillo ran off: Armadillo 1, Nick 0.

Then I bumped it up to a marathon a day with two rest days a week in February. They were slow marathons, usually over five hours; I would almost always walk the uphills. My legs hurt so bad that month I had to walk 10 miles on my rest days just to shake it off. Within a week, I stopped driving to my local training spot at Turkey Mountain and started running there. Being six miles from my house, it instantly added 12 miles to my day. *Why drive to your running spot, when you can run to your running spot?*

Turkey Mountain is not a mountain at all. It's 300 acres of "wilderness" in the middle of Tulsa, Oklahoma, and is better described as a big wooded lot in a hilly, rocky part of town with some power lines running through it. The highest point of the park isn't even 900 feet above sea level. The majority of Tulsa is around 700 feet above sea level. So as you can see, it's certainly a monstrosity of a mountain to train on. But it's Turkey. It's the best trail system we have in Tulsa. You can easily clock five miles running the perimeter; it has some decent views of the Arkansas River, and there are plenty of intertwining trails to mix things up.

Later that month, a snow and ice storm blew in. Our hilly neighborhood essentially shut down. We couldn't get our cars out, although we never actually tried. *My other car is a pair of shoes now; who needs an engine and four wheels?* I literally ran our errands for about a week. Kitchen faucet breaks? Run to Home Depot with a bag, run back with the faucet on your back. Need some groceries? Run to the store, come back with celery sticking out your backpack side pockets.

I started reading books about thru-hiking and FKTs. Books like *North, Free Outside,* and *Thirst.* One of the most impactful books was *Mud, Rocks, Blazes* by Heather Anderson. I studied it like a textbook. I underlined and dog-eared the pages. I took notes. She had the know-how, and I wanted to know how, too.

A marathon a day for a month. If you ever choose to run a marathon a day for a month, choose February on a non-leap year. Even in the shortest month of the year, my legs were on fire. I soaked in more hot baths during those 28 days than I had in my entire adult life. I couldn't sit still; my legs had become restless and fidgety. It hurt too bad to stop moving.

In March, it was time to progress. The western end of the Ouachita Trail (OT) is about three hours away from Tulsa. It's 223 miles long and stretches from Talihina, Oklahoma, to Little Rock, Arkansas. The men's supported record was 3 days, 4 hours, and 34 minutes. *How am I supposed to break the 2,650-mile PCT record if I can't break this measly 223-mile record?*

The weather was only going to get hotter in Oklahoma, so I decided to go after the OT FKT while it was still cool out. I wanted the self-supported record, but I wanted to beat the supported record at the same time. It would take 75-mile days to break it. I had done 73 miles in a day before, just for fun. And by this point, I was running for five-plus hours most days. Somehow, those were enough numbers to convince myself I could do it. *I run a marathon a day. I've got this. I don't have to run the whole trail, just like half of it.*

What a naive, innocent fool I was. I clearly didn't have any clue what it takes to cross 223 miles in three days on this kind of terrain, but ignorance on fire is better than knowledge on ice—sometimes.

I started asking questions about the OT on a Facebook group, and Kristy Dodd asked if I'd like some support on my FKT attempt. *Why not?* She was the maintenance coordinator for the OT; she knew everything about it. She had hiked across the United States several times and even volunteered at 100-mile races. She was one of those people who flew under the radar but clearly knew what she was doing in this space. Despite originally wanting to go after a self-supported record, I figured if someone with her background was offering to help, I should take advantage of it. And so Kristy became my resupply team and a trusted friend.

On the first weekend of March, I gave the supported OT FKT a go. And I failed. Miserably. I only made it 51 miles before quitting at Queen Wilhelmina State Park at the top of Rich Mountain, the second-tallest mountain in Arkansas. My inner thighs were beyond chafing—they were *bleeding*.

I tried again the next week. In fifteen hours, I crossed the same 51 miles but was lying down next to the state park bathroom, puking uncontrollably all night long. I couldn't hold down fluids. *I don't know how these ultrarunners run 100 miles through mountain terrain in one go, but I'm going to figure it out.*

I tried again a week later. That time, I stopped after throwing up blood near the same spot.

The difference between hiking 50 miles and running 50 miles is astounding.

The following weekend, I tried the OT again. I eased myself out of my car and limped to the starting line. My knee had been bothering me since the previous attempt. Kristy's eyes said one thing, but her smile said the other. At mile 16, she made me stop, "You're done. It's not worth risking a permanent injury." This was the same day Fawn Hernandez started her FKT attempt on the Ouachita Trail. I saw her support crew drive by, but I was too embarrassed to attempt meeting her. She set a new record after completing the entire 223-mile trail in 3 days, 22 hours, and 14 minutes—an extremely high bar for the women's supported FKT—all on her first attempt. And there I was getting off the trail at mile 16, on my fourth attempt. Talk about demoralizing.

I gave it one more go, one week later—this time by myself. I had already asked Kristy to support me on multiple failed attempts. And she did help, graciously and without complaint, but I couldn't keep doing that to her. She had given me enough of her time; I couldn't ask for more. Since I was solo, I was back to a self-supported FKT attempt, still going for the overall record.

It ended up being a complete bust. With each step, my legs grew heavier. My foot hurt. My knee hurt. My hamstring hurt. My calf hurt. My quads hurt. I slogged forward in achy misery for 46 miles before throwing in the towel. I wasn't having fun at all. I felt like the more I ran, the worse at it I became. Five days later, I found out I had given myself a stress fracture on my left foot. I ran on it in pain for 30 miles before stopping. *What am I doing with my life!!??*

So at that point, I had to stay off my foot—doctor's orders. No strenuous activities on my feet for six to eight weeks. *Let's see if we can make that five to seven.*

Four weeks in, I was riding my bicycle across town to get my errands done in an attempt to stay in shape. By week five, I was in Southern Utah attempting to hike small trails. I started a two-mile hike with crutches and a boot on. Within a quarter mile, I left the boot and crutches on the side of the trail to pick up on my way back. I quickly learned my foot wasn't ready, and I bailed on the rest of the trip.

When I got home, I was in the dumps. I had dedicated my entire 2021 to this goal, and here I was, barely able to walk a couple of city blocks without my foot throbbing. To give myself a bigger window to focus and train, I put other responsibilities on the back burner. I was neglecting priorities like property maintenance, employee benefit accounts, and family. I even lost a friend because "I wasn't hanging out with him enough." It felt like I was making negative progress. It felt like I was wasting my time.

A few weeks later, I went back to Utah to get my mind right. To get back in the scenery that inspires me to keep going. I told myself I was going for "footless adventures." I kayaked down the Green River through Labyrinth Canyon outside Canyonlands National Park. I went canyoneering: rappelling off 100-foot walls into slot canyons, squeezing through cracks, and escaping car-sized holes full of stagnant water. That's "footless," right? Hanging from a rope? (Let's be honest, the adventures weren't really that "footless.")

But there was good news: My foot finally wasn't hurting. So I kept heading west. On my way to the Lake Tahoe area of the PCT, I stopped near Salt Lake City. I decided to put a little more foot back into the mix and went for a 20k run through American Fork Canyon. My foot didn't hurt, not even a little. *Am I back?* (I talked to myself in kilometers, so I'd feel like I was going farther on my first run since the injury.)

Outside Lake Tahoe, I ran back and forth from Donner Pass on the PCT. Twenty-five miles with my pack and overnight gear for extra weight. I was worn out. Winded. Out of shape. Or was it the elevation? Or was it both?

I pushed to turn them into 50-mile runs over the next week, but I was stuck at 30 to 40-mile days. I didn't have the energy to go past 40. I wasn't used to it anymore. And I didn't like it. Somehow I had convinced myself that I could run 50 miles on a regular basis at this point, even though I was just recovering from breaking my foot on a 50-mile run.

I traveled north toward the Olympic Peninsula. I wanted to get close to the Blue Glacier. I didn't think I could day hike it when Hannah and I came through here the previous year, but times had changed. The viewpoint of the glacier was 40 miles round-trip. By the time I crossed the first 20 miles and saw the glacier, I could see the top of Mount Olympus. At 7,980 feet, it's the tallest peak in the range. I certainly didn't plan to go all the way up to the top when I started that morning, but I could see a trail through the snow guiding the way. *It's right there. I'm already here. Why not?*

It took five hours to posthole six miles round-trip through knee-high snow all the way to the top and back down to the moraine, where I originally had planned to stop. But that summit—Mount Olympus—it was something else. The traverse over the blue glacier, staring into the heart of it through a crevasse. The sheer power was mesmerizing. An infinite chasm that faded from vibrant light to dark blue and eventually to black. I could feel the glacier breathing. *Don't get too close, though—it'll swallow you whole.* And then the avalanche fields and endless views from the top. I could see into Canada, toward Mount Rainier, and even the Pacific Ocean.

Maybe I still have this in me. I had an absolute blast climbing Mount Olympus. I wasn't pushing hard on it. I was just hiking it for fun, taking my time. Running when I felt like running, hiking when I felt like hiking. Despite the fact that I carried a fully loaded bag for extra weight and didn't make it back to the van until 2:00 a.m., I didn't consider it a training run. It felt more like a fun stroll through the woods.

I stopped by the Olympic National Park Wilderness Center in Port Angeles to look for more high-mileage running days. I decided to get an overnight permit for somewhere deep in the Olympics. I figured I could run in 40–50 miles, stay a night, and then run back the next day.

I leaned on the counter across from the Park Ranger to plan out where I'd camp. He told me the mountain passes were still buried under snow. I'd need an ice axe and crampons to traverse them. "If you're trying to get in high-mileage days like that, it's just not the right time of year for the Olympics. The snow levels don't get manageable here until July, usually." *Should I tell him I just day hiked to the top of Mount Olympus, without an ice axe, in shorts and a t-shirt?*

"What about the coastline?" I pointed to the north and south coasts of Olympic National Park along the Pacific Ocean on the map. "There's no snow there. That looks like 40–50 miles. I could run that, camp, and then run back?"

"On paper it looks like a good idea, but it's impossible. I've tried to do it myself before. It's just not possible to do the entire coast in one day. First, you'll be fighting the tides. You have to cross tidal headlands during low tide; otherwise, you'll get trapped out in the Pacific. You end up having to camp and wait for the tides to change before you can keep moving. And besides that, you can't even cross the Quillayute or Hoh Rivers. They aren't fordable. You'd have to arrange a boat ride or go miles inland, just to get to a bridge to cross and then come back to the coast."

"Can you swim across them?"

"Both rivers are all glacier melt."

Well fine.

I still went to the coast—not for 50 miles, but to touch the ocean. I picked up a few rocks and wrote why I was running on them. Five rocks for five reasons to run. They became my training rocks. I'd throw them in my pack for extra weight, reinforcing the reasons I had set out on this mission to thru-hike the PCT faster than anyone's ever done before.

Next, I shot over to the PCT in the North Cascades, Snoqualmie

Pass. I wanted to get my feet back on the PCT, figure out if I still had this in me or not since the Mount Olympus day hike went so well. When I pulled into the parking lot, I saw piles of snow as tall as my van. I could barely see the top of the trailhead sign hiding under the drifts. *Great. There's more snow here than in the Olympics. But I'm already here. Might as well see how far I can make it.* Within three miles, I fell through a snow bridge, six feet into an ice-cold mountain stream. I climbed out, shivering cold and wet, and slogged my way back to the van. *Never mind. How am I supposed to get high-mileage days in when I'm falling through holes in the snow the whole way?*

I started working my way back east, toward Oklahoma. I stopped to explore the mountains of Idaho and ran the Grand Sawtooth Loop, a 73-mile trek through some of the best parts of the Sawtooths, in two days—with rocks in my pack. My jaw dropped. *Why does no one talk about this place?* The peaks are jagged and sharp, like serrated saw blades. Sheer granite carved by ancient glaciers. Rugged to the point where no building can be built. Uninhabitable the majority of the year, so it wards off the weak and maintains its purity. It was much drier than I expected, though; the trails were dusty and hot.

But one of our renters called while I was in the Sawtooths. The grout in one of their bathrooms had apparently failed some time ago, and one of the tiles had fallen off the shower wall. They were down to just one functional shower. "I'm out of town right now, but I'm en route back to Oklahoma. I can be back and start working on it in four or so days."

But you can't just drive past the Wind River Range without checking them out. *Just one day. I'll just run into the Titcomb Basin and back. It'll just take one day.* Thirty-six miles, all over 9,000 feet above sea level, and a whole bunch of fun later, I was back at the van. The last time I hiked this trail, last June, also with snow—from the Elk Hart Park trailhead to the end of the Titcomb Basin and back—it took all day, from 5:20 a.m. to 9:00 p.m. And I came back sore with bloody, blistered heels. This time it only took eight and a half hours—with three days of food, a full sleep kit, and rocks in my pack for extra weight. I even took the time to explore a glacier cave. And I felt fresh. I felt like I could have kept going. I wasn't even trying to do it fast; I was just enjoying my time. I was encouraged. I knew I was getting faster.

I remember having a conversation with a group of backpackers near the end of the run. Their minds were blown that I was running to the Titcomb basin and back in a day.

"It took us three days just to get to the basin!"

"Well, in your defense, you're carrying a much heavier pack. You came to spend a week out here. I came to run it in a day."

Jokingly, one of them asked, "Are you training to run across America or something?"

"Actually, yes. Yes, I am." I explained my PCT FKT dreams.

"This is crazy. You're 30 miles into a day run, in mountain terrain, it's barely noon, and you don't even look tired."

"The mountains give me energy."

Then one of them interjected, "You have a gift." Those four words have stuck with me ever since. They raised my belief. I was only six months into this new sport and was already relishing in 30-plus-mile mountain runs. *Maybe I do have a gift.*

By the time I finished remodeling the shower in the rent house back in Oklahoma, it was nearly July. I had planned to start the PCT on August 15th. I'd start at the Canadian border and go south to try to beat the snow in the Sierra while missing the worst of the heat in the desert. I only had a month and a half before go time, and despite a handful of successful runs out west, I didn't feel ready. A few good runs spread out over a couple of weeks isn't the same as 45-mile days back-to-back for two months in a row.

Timothy Olson, a well-known ultrarunner, had recently started an attempt to break the supported FKT record on the PCT. To give perspective on how solid of a runner this guy is, he ran the Western States 100-mile race in 14 hours and 46 minutes. *One hundred miles in 14 hours—WHAT???* I was following his PCT journey online. He made a comment, "My entire running career, everything has led me to this moment." He even had sponsors. *His entire running career? I've only been running for six months.*

I started messaging Joe "Stringbean" McConaughy several months prior. I had reached out to him for some advice about the PCT since he had previously broken the supported PCT FKT a few years back. I didn't know he was a coach at the time.

"Are you looking for a running coach, or are you just looking for advice? I'd be glad to help with either."

I was initially just looking for advice, and he gave me tons of it. But now it was time to take it to the next level.

I sent him an email: "OK, OK, take my money. I obviously need coaching help to achieve my goal. I thought I was invincible until I started running." *I'm over here breaking my feet trying to train like Karel Sabbe, and Timothy Olson is already halfway through running the entire PCT.*

The training Joe scheduled for me was spot-on. Instead of my self-prescribed marathon-a-day training plan, I had rest days. There were speed runs, hill sprints, strength training, long runs, and even days dedicated to just hiking. I wasn't constantly tearing my body down; there was plenty of time to heal. My muscles were growing in power. Muscles I didn't even know existed were getting worked. I was feeling strong. More importantly, I was feeling healthy.

A couple of weeks before my planned start date, I went out to spend some time on the PCT in the Southern California desert. Put my feet on the trail. Get my mind right. Train where I'd be attempting the speed record. I'd put two gallons of water in my backpack for extra weight and run 15–30 miles up the trail before turning back to repeat the same miles in the opposite direction.

But then a fire popped up on the PCT. Then another. And another. New fire closures were sprouting by the day—and here I was, just two weeks away from starting this journey.

Even before all these new fires ignited, I had been struggling with how to get around the Lionshead Fire closure in Oregon, the remnants of a bad fire from the previous year. About 20 miles of trail were closed, and the only way around it—because of how big the fire was—was adding on an extra 100 miles of road walk. When the report came out about how Timothy Olson got through, I was shocked. *Oh, snap. He got in a car?* He ended up taking a car ride around it and added on mileage by going back and forth on the trail to make up for the difference. There's no way I can pull that off and qualify for the self-supported record.

The Dixie Fire grew. It consumed nearly a million acres of forest in California. And with it came a 100-mile trail closure. *How am I supposed to get around that?* The fires were out of control, and it was only the beginning of fire season.

And so the toughest question of the year surfaced. *Is it even possible to do the PCT now?*

I emailed Joe. I called friends. I asked Google. Should I do a different trail? Should I still attempt? What would be the consequences if I just ran through the Lionshead Fire Closure anyway? There's not technically a fire there anymore; I'd just be dealing with a bunch of downed trees and sketchy debris. Do they even monitor this area? *Ah… there's a $5,000 fine for violating one of these fire closures.* OK, never mind.

The fires got worse. They spread, they raged, they tore apart small mountain towns. Closures got bigger. Smoke was traveling from California to New York.

The decision was made. The PCT was a no-go.

With my head held low, I drove back home. I had prepped, trained, and geared up for this event all year long. My resupply boxes were even already packed. But I counted my blessings. Some people's livelihoods were being completely burned to the ground near the PCT. If the hardest task for me was deciding I couldn't hike a trail, I didn't really have it that bad. But I didn't want to let all this preparation go to waste. *I'll just go after a different trail.*

And so the last-minute decision was made to change from the Pacific Crest Trail to the Pacific Northwest Trail.

The PNT traverses 1,248 miles, east to west, across three of my favorite national parks: Olympic and North Cascades in Washington and, of course, Glacier in Montana. *That'll be fun.*

I knew nothing else about the PNT. I didn't know how rugged it was. I didn't know there were sections of it with class 3 scrambles or that you have to bushwhack through forests with no trail at all.

I had no idea what I was getting myself into.

With the limited time I had before starting the trail, I decided to skip planning the finer details like I had with the PCT. I just focused on mapping my resupply points—as long as I knew where I could pick up more food, I could figure out the rest along the way. As I looked at the map to determine where my resupply points would be, I noticed the western end of the trail followed the coast of Washington in Olympic National Park. *Oh, that will be fun!* Hannah and I had explored a few areas along this coast when we were in our van; it's a beautiful place.

And then it dawned on me.

Just two months prior, a park ranger at the Wilderness Center in Olympic National Park was telling me how it wasn't possible to complete the entire north and south coasts of the park in a day because of the tides and the rivers. And here I was, discovering that the same 40-mile stretch of coastline that park ranger was talking about was my first 40 miles of the PNT.

Some might imagine the toughest part of the Olympic Coast to be the soft sand that sinks under your feet, the slippery boulders you have to cross, or even the near-vertical cliffs you have to climb up and over. But the real challenge is beating the tides. That's not so much of a hurdle for people taking their time, but to cross the biggest coastal section of this trail in one day would be quite the trick.

A few places along the coast have "headlands," areas that are only passable during low tide. Imagine a coastal cliff. At low tide there's a beach section where you can walk across to the other side. During high tide, that sand is underwater, and waves crash against the bluffs. So the trick, especially with doing the entire coast in one day, is timing the tides right. If you don't, you could be stuck waiting upwards of 6–18 hours before that same area is passable again. Or worse, if you're crossing a headland when high tide comes in, you could end up swimming in the Pacific. I didn't know if anyone had ever done it before. That park ranger certainly didn't think it was possible. The current FKT holder, Jeff Garmire, spent two nights on the coast, partially because of the tides.

I questioned myself. *How can I—a rookie, a novice, a brand-new hiker—be going after one of Jeff Garmire's records?* He's hiked more than 30,000 miles and has well over a dozen FKT records. I had never even thru-hiked before.

But there's a fascinating science and pattern to the way the moon pulls the ocean, and I was determined to crack the code. *If I study anything about the PNT, it'll be the tides.* I spent days scribbling on tide charts, calendars, and maps. I picked August 23rd as my start date because it had the best window of tides in a two-month time period. If crossing the entire coast in one day was going to happen, it'd have to be on this day.

I drew a map of the coast with the time frames so I could visualize which parts of the coast had to be crossed during what hours. The tides and the mileage didn't line up conveniently, but if I really hustled and got lucky it might be possible. It wasn't going to be easy, but it was possible. And possible was all I needed.

THE COAST

MY EYES OPEN before my alarm goes off. I check the time: 3:37 a.m.
My alarm is going to go off in eight minutes. I'm anxious, excited,
and alert. Today's the day.

I lie there next to Hannah and think about the day ahead. We're
in a $25 Walmart tent camped at Lake Ozette in Olympic National
Park. The three-mile spur trail that connects with the PNT is within
walking distance of the campground. The plan is to be on that spur
trail by 4:30. My backpack is already packed and ready to go. All I
have to do is cook breakfast, make some coffee, and slip my shoes and
socks on before I say goodbye.

The alarm goes off. I sit up, stretch and yawn. I pull back the quilt
and hear Hannah ask, "Is it time?" I whisper back, "It's time."

I creep out of the tent, walk over to the car, and grab my stove, a
pot, bacon, crescent rolls, and coffee. As I sit down at the picnic table,
I look out over Lake Ozette. The sky is clear. The stars and moon are
reflecting on the water. It's a crisp 50 degrees out. I pull the hood on
my jacket over my head. As I fire up the stove to boil some water, I
hear Hannah getting out of the tent. *God, I'm going to miss her.* This
is the last time I get to see her until she picks me up on the other end
of the PNT in 30 or so days.

As the water finishes boiling, I see Hannah putting our car camping
supplies in the car. Last night she insisted on packing everything away

in the morning so I could focus on getting ready. I mix the instant coffee and heat up the bacon and rolls. This is going to be my last hot meal for a while. *I'm going to savor it.*

Fog hangs low over the far end of the lake. A doe and fawn munch on tall grass about 25 feet away. A rabbit sits only a few feet from our tent. The fog on the lake rolls forward, signaling it's time to get moving. I finish eating the last piece of bacon and pack the stove away in the car. In an effort to save my legs as much as possible, Hannah drives me to the trailhead, less than a quarter mile away. We say our goodbyes, and I walk into the woods toward the coast.

The fire closure reroute near Glacier National Park is almost three miles shorter than the original route, so I need to add on three miles somewhere to make sure I put forth an equal effort on the FKT. As I reach the sign that indicates 3.1 miles to the western terminus of the PNT, Cape Alava, I snap a photo and start the clock for the FKT attempt. It's 4:37 a.m. I have to use this spur trail to access the PNT anyway, might as well start the clock here and keep my effort on the PNT one continuous footpath.

Less than an hour later, I smell saltwater in the wind coming off the Pacific. I feel the ocean's aura. The sound of the waves is rejuvenating. Despite the darkness, I sense a break in the trees. The forest has come to an end. I step up onto a large pile of driftwood and see the ocean. I've reached the beginning of the PNT. Now's time for the fun to begin.

I tell myself to not focus on pictures or views. I've hiked this portion of the coast before. *Just make good time while not twisting an ankle on day one.* My head is down, attuned to my foot placement as I jog/hop from rock to rock. All of a sudden, I hear an animal up ahead. I glance up to see a black bear running away from me on the coast, not even 50 feet away. *Their butts are so fluffy!* I quickly pull out my phone to snap a picture. By the time I get my camera ready, the bear has climbed up the bluff and turned back to look at me. We watch each other for a couple of minutes before moving on. *What a start to the PNT! So much for not being focused on pictures or views.*

A few hours later, I'm making good time on hard sand, a convenience that usually only appears during super low tides. The weather is perfect. I'm smiling and having the time of my life. Suddenly, I see something bright orange on the side of a rock. As I get closer, it becomes obvious—it's a starfish! I stop to take a picture and then see several more of its spiny-skinned cousins inside a tide pool. I keep moving, but within a quarter mile I'm distracted again. A galaxy of purple and orange sea stars is clumped together on the side of a sea stack as if having a party that I wasn't invited to. *Exploring may be my downfall. I'm running around all giggly like a little kid, finding dozens of starfish and sea urchins—while I'm supposed to be setting a speed record.*

Not too long afterward I'm climbing through an ocean-carved rock arch. I'm still getting sidetracked. *But it'll only take two minutes! I haven't crawled through this one before!*

The Olympic Coast is a magical place. I can only imagine finishing the PNT right here, like most PNT thru-hikers do. Crossing the continental divide, seven different mountain ranges, and over 1,200 miles to get to the fresh, crisp ocean air. And then spending a few days on the coastline, camping on the beach, playing on the bluffs, soaking in all the glory. Part of me wishes I was ending on the coast. Part of me wishes I could take my time. But I'm going after a speed record, and starting on the coast during this one specific hour of this one specific day could make all the difference with the tides. *How much time would it take to do this place justice anyway?* I just spent the previous week on and off the coast, scouting the tides and headlands. Now I'm spending an entire day on it, dark to dark. I've even been out here on previous trips before, and I'm still left wanting more.

Rocks. Sea stacks. Cliffs protruding out into the ocean. The sound of the waves splashing up against the rocks. The smell of saltwater in the air. It's one of the most unique trails I've ever been on. There's actually not much of a trail at all, except for through a few small forest sections. You just follow the coastline for over 40 miles—from rocks to sand to cliffs to forest—all with the Pacific right by your side.

I come upon a massive downed tree on the coast that I'll have to navigate around; it's too big to climb over. The root end is acting like a net, catching a mass of seaweed. A thin layer of the green sea slime coats the beach surrounding it. This whole area is obviously underwater during high tide; everything is slick and wet. I walk across the sheets of kelp, being careful not to slip on any of the rocks under it. It's mostly a balancing act; it's impossible to get any traction on the slick mess. *It's day one, and I'm already wishing I brought my trekking poles.*

I had made a last-minute decision to not bring my poles on the PNT because of all the road walks. I typically only use my poles on stream crossings and steep climbs. I like to have my hands free, and it seemed like I would be carrying the poles more than using them—so they got left behind.

Phwoop.

My foot slips off a rock and sinks deep into a green spaghetti pit. I catch myself from falling over, but I'm instantly up to my knees in a saltwatery seaweed soup. I've discovered a tide pool hidden by a cloak of smelly, rotting, thick, floating sea-skin. I climb out of the pool and wipe the slime off my hands onto my shorts. (Little did I know that my shorts would become my hand towel for the next 1,200 miles.)

A few miles later, I turn the corner around a bluff. I see the popular Hole-in-the-Wall arch, a giant rock wall that protrudes out into the ocean with one large hole in it that you can walk through only during low tide. The beach is suddenly crowded with people. I'm nearing the Quillayute River, my halfway point for the day, where one of the biggest rivers on the Olympic Peninsula dumps into the Pacific Ocean.

The Quillayute River isn't fordable, and it's all glacier melt, so you wouldn't want to swim it either. You either have to road walk nine miles around the river to a bridge and back to the coast, or you can catch a boat ride across it. Most westbound hikers will catch a boat ride from a fisherman at the La Push Marina on the south side of the river. That's certainly the more enjoyable way to get across. Me? I'm headed the opposite direction. There's no marina on this side of the river. I'm doing what any FKTer wants to do. I'm going all the way around it, adding on more miles.

A few miles later, I'm walking past a gas station. All of a sudden,

I find myself inside it, holding a Dr Pepper. I look at the checkout line. Four people. *I have to wait for four people to check out before I can buy this? Maybe I should just put it back in the fridge and leave. This is killing my time.* I grab a Mountain Dew. I might as well have two cold carbonated beverages if I'm going to put up with this wait. One, two, three, and then four people check out. I step up to the counter, and a family of three from around the corner starts yelling, "It's our turn to check out! We were here first." I didn't see them until now, but, whatever. It'll probably take less time to just let them check out than have an entire conversation about who was here first. *I shouldn't have come in here. It's been 10 minutes.* They place all their snacks and drinks on the counter in the slowest manner possible. *Are they purposefully slowing me down? Who told them I'm trying to set an FKT?* I joke with myself, realizing they aren't going slower than normal; I'm just trying to do everything super fast.

Before I get back to the ocean, both my fizzy drinks are gone. That's OK. I drank them fast on purpose. Who wants a flat pop after it's been jostled around in a pocket for a few dozen miles anyway? *Drink them while they are fresh and cold, then throw them away in the trash cans near the beach trailhead. You might not see any other trash cans until Port Townsend, 200 miles away.* Ain't no way I'm carrying two extra empty bottles for four more days!

Back on trail. It's flat, open, and clear. The trees are tall. It smells fresh. I'm getting closer to the ocean again. I start running. The flat run turns into a gentle downhill cruise. It's fast, easy, and fun. It's energizing. Luckily, people can hear me running from behind them, and they kindly step off the trail to let me pass. *There are so many people near these trailheads.* Back on the beach. Then time to go up and over another cliff. Ropes and rope ladders help to ascend and descend the steep bluffs. *It's an obstacle course!* A line of people wait to use a rope on the right to climb up this bluff. One person is about halfway up the rope, making it look incredibly harder than it has to be. They are barely moving—struggling with every inch. I see a rope on the left not even being used. I ask, "What's wrong with the rope on the left?"

No one in line seems to know.

One person blurts, "No one has been using it."

As I step out of line toward the rope on the left, I shout, "I'll test it out for you guys!" I'm up and on top of the cliff before the person using the rope on the right is even three-quarters of the way up. Half the line moves over to the rope on the left. *I started a movement!*

There's a bottleneck of people on the other side of this rope section waiting to go down, and I have to get around it. A group of hikers step to the side of the trail after one of them shouts, "Hey, let's let this guy get by!" *Was my impatience showing that much? I guess that's OK because it worked. Ha!*

I start to wonder if the rope on the left is supposed to be for people to go down on. One rope to go down, one rope to climb up. Did I just make the bottleneck worse? *Meh, they weren't even using the rope on the left anyway.*

As I'm running down the steep slope back toward the beach on the other side of the bluff, an older gentleman chuckles, "All the way to Oil City in a day?" I respond back with, "That's actually the plan." Oil City isn't a city at all. To locals, it's a small off-grid community left over from a failed petroleum extraction site from the late 19th century; the terrain was determined to be too rugged for development. To me, it's just a dirt parking lot at the end of a logging road where I'll be exiting the coast. It's where I'll begin heading inland along the Hoh River to start crossing the Olympic Mountains. *I hope I can time the tides right and actually make it all the way to Oil City today.*

As I come back down off the cliffs toward the beach, I see it's still high tide. I was hoping to catch the low end of high tide here so I could pass the Scott's Bluff area without waiting for the water to go back down, but I'm early. High tide is still too high. The beach isn't passable. It could be two or more hours before it becomes passable again.

I look for other options around the flooded corner; I see a potential route up a cliff. *There's a crack.* Instinctively, one of my hands goes into the crack. The other on a root. I lift myself off the ground and twist my foot in the crack to get another point of contact. Now both hands are in the crack. Now I'm using another root. Here's a foothold. There's a foothold. I carefully climb up to the top and slowly work my way down the other side. *High tide ain't gonna stop me!*

I'm back on a beach-walk portion, but there's not much room to walk between the bluffs, boulders, and waves. When a wave comes in to crash against the cliff, I jump up on a rock to avoid getting wet. When the waves go back out, I run a few yards on the sand, trying to beat the next wave. I repeat this maneuver a few times before a wave finally catches my feet. *Dang it. My feet were almost dry!*

Salty, sandy, ocean-soaked shoes—what more could you ask for? It's OK, though. I have a plan for this. I'm wearing an older pair of shoes on purpose; I have new shoes and socks cached at the end of this coastal section, so I won't have to deal with sand in my shoes the rest of the trip. *No matter what, I'll have dry socks and shoes at some point tomorrow.*

I keep moving along the coast, still trying to beat the waves. I have to get through this headland as close to high tide as possible because the next hard tide to catch is at Diamond Rock, over 10 miles away, and I need time to get there before the peak of low tide. That headland requires the lowest tide of the entire coast to cross, so the window of the tide being low enough is extremely narrow—it's usually only passable once a day, and sometimes it can even be impassable for several days at a time.

I run into a father and son hiking in the opposite direction. "How's the tide that way?" I ask.

The father points to a cliff behind them, "We actually just had to wait for 30 minutes on the other side of that wall for the water to go down. You have to hop across on rocks for part of it, but it's doable now."

I thank them for the information and tell them about the route I took to climb over the bluff not too far behind me in case it's still flooded when they get there. *Wow. The timing for this tide could not have been more perfect. I'm catching it within moments of it becoming passable.*

Left foot, right foot, left foot, right foot. Sandy beaches. Pebbly beaches. Seaweedy beaches. Rocks, boulders, rocks—and to no one's surprise—even more rocks. Up and over more bluffs with fun ropes and ladders and back onto another beach again. I need to go left, to the south. But there's an arch keyhole to the right, and it's so inviting. Looking through the arch, you can see the sun coming closer to setting over the ocean bluffs, sea stacks, and headlands jetting out into the water. I hurry over and climb through. *I'm running late to catch my Diamond Rock tide window, and I'm over here climbing through a keyhole in the wrong direction.* I shake my head and get back on track. I keep moving south.

An hour later, I'm crossing through the Mosquito Creek campground, the last camping area before the Diamond Rock headland. Someone asks me where I'm headed. It'll be dark soon. I tell them I'm trying to make it to Oil City tonight. They ask, "Are you trying to make it across at the next low tide?"

"Yeah."

"Isn't that at 7:00?"

I look down at my watch; it's 6:43. I have 17 minutes till the peak of low tide and five more miles to go. "Yeah… I've got to hurry!"

Camping at Mosquito Creek was my original plan if I didn't think I could catch the last tide. It's going to be close, but if I'm going to make it through this tide window, I don't have time to hesitate. I need to run.

The trail through the woods on top of this coastal bluff is slick and muddy. There's a fine line between running too hard, turning the muck into a treadmill, and moving too slowly. It's getting dark. It's humid. My clothes are drenched in sweat. My fingers are so wet I struggle to operate my phone screen to check my location compared to the time. Up and down, through the trees and across creeks. I skip taking the time to refill my water bottles because I don't want to miss my tide window.

When I finally descend the cliffs back down to the beach, I come across another rope ladder. Most of these hanging steps are on 45–70 degree inclines to help with footing. Not this one, though. This one becomes so steep I have to turn around and face it. It's become vertical. *This is an actual freaking ladder I'm climbing down. Oh fun… and it's missing three steps.*

Back to running. I finally see the Diamond Rock headland; it's on the other side of a crescent-shaped beach. As I work my way around, I realize I'll have to climb over boulders to get through it. Five minutes later, I'm wondering if this is what everyone has to deal with or if there's sometimes an actual beach you can walk across if the tide is lower. Either way, this is what I've got, and it's making for some slow progress.

Everything is slick. Some boulders are the size of cars. Some are even bigger remnants that fell off the cliff above. Some are the size of beach balls. The higher I climb, the drier the boulders become, which makes for faster movement, but then I have more climbing up and down to do, and I'm not sure if it's faster or if I'm just using more energy.

The boulders and rocks begin to shrink until I'm clearly back on another beach. Only this one is disappearing. It's already a few inches underwater. *I'm about to completely lose my tide window.* When a wave comes in from the right, it ripples across the sinking beach all the way to the cliff on the left. I slosh through the rising waters. *I've got to hurry.*

It's pitch black out and beginning to rain, but I suddenly see a dry beach a few feet higher in the distance. *I know where I'm at now. That's the bank of the Hoh River.* This is the end of the coast. It's time to follow the river back inland toward the Oil City trailhead.

I scouted this area a few days ago during daylight, so I know the trail exiting the beach doesn't follow the line on my map. Part of the river bank must have drastically changed during a river flooding at some point. It looks completely different in the dark now too. *Thank goodness I scouted this area. It'd be hard to find the trail that exits the beach in the dark for the first time.* I still struggle to find the beach/river bank exit. After a few attempts at getting off the beach, I finally find the trail. *Back in business.*

By 9:00 p.m., I've set up camp on the side of a dirt road next to where I had cached my dry shoes, socks, and an orange Gatorade. I chug the Gatorade and quickly regret it. My stomach starts to turn. *Dang it. Don't throw up.* I drank that way too fast. I try to subside the nausea and lie down under my tarp. Bad idea. Within minutes I'm crawling out to throw up. My upper body is out from under the tarp, my legs still under it, orange fluid is spewing. *I didn't even make it 24 hours without puking.* I instantly feel better, though.

I check my mileage—49.2 miles, and I've crossed the entire coast in one day. Day one is a success.

THE CHAFING

MY SHORTS ARE STILL SOAKED from yesterday. *I'll just wear the dry underwear I slept in. They look like compression shorts anyway.* I'm on my feet and moving shortly after 6:00 a.m. I must have slept through my alarm. *I guess I needed it. Ha! Day one, and I already need it? That's not a good sign.*

Today consists of gravel-logging roads for around 30 miles until I get back into Olympic National Park to start crossing the Olympic Mountains. The roads are mundane compared to the coast, but it's peaceful. I'm the only one out here it seems.

When I get back to cell service, I have several business calls to return and emails to send. *I guess I can't go two days on the PNT without working.* Before starting the trail, I changed my voicemail and set an autoresponder on my email to redirect any business calls to other channels, but no. Some people persist. And so I return the calls, and I send the emails. But I do it while I'm moving.

Not too much later, I'm walking down another dirt road, and I check the map. *Crap. I'm not on trail. How the hell did I get off-trail?* I missed a turn 1.3 miles back. I've been so careful about checking the map at every junction. The turns out here aren't marked for the PNT, so you have to check. *How did I not see that turn? Oh, right, I was replying to emails.*

By midafternoon, it's hotter outside than I'd like. These roads have no shade. I'm drenched in sweat, and chafing is already becoming a major problem. *This isn't fair.* I spent so much time this year trying out different fabrics, topicals, and methods to prevent my thighs from rubbing raw. And here I am, on day two of this journey, with thunder thighs of fire.

I stop at Bogachiel State Park to take a quick shower, dry off my clothes, and doctor the nether regions. Between the light rain last night and the ocean's humidity on day one, about half of my kit is wet. I spend longer than I should—well over two hours sitting outside the campground bathroom waiting for my gear to dry and devices to charge—secretly hoping the chafing will somehow magically heal before having to get going again.

The Chafing. Ha! More like "The Shining." This is a real-life horror story.

After a few more miles of gravel roads, someone pulls over in their car and asks, "Want a ride to the trailhead?" I stop walking. I look at him. I look down at my feet and then back up and sigh, "Yeah, I'd love a ride." He motions to get in his car. "But I'm doing this all by foot. I appreciate it, though."

Now the rash of rub is spreading under my arms and even on my lower back. Despite drying my gear off at Bogachiel State Park, my clothes are already saturated with sweat. I'm walking with a wide-legged waddle walk in an attempt to keep my thighs from getting any worse. I dangle a carrot in front of myself: *Once I get back on a foot trail in the mountains, there will be tons of shade. It'll be cooler there.*

By the time I make it to the Bogachiel River Trail, I've taken my shirt off. It's dramatically helping with the chafing under my arms. More airflow—that area has a chance to dry now that there's not a sopping wet shirt sleeve draped under my arm rubbing up and down. But now my shoulders are taking a beating from my backpack straps.

I'm wearing a running belt for extra storage access on the go. I turn it around to grab my evening food. It's drenched. *Has my waist belt been collecting all the sweat coming down off my back?* I keep hiking while grabbing what I need out of it. I feel sweat dripping off the bottom of my backpack and hitting the back of my legs as I'm walking now.

There's a consistent drip every 30 seconds. *Wow. Am I really sweating that much?* Now that my bum bag is off my backside and the sweat is dripping down off my pack, instead of collecting and channeling down my butt crack, I feel a significant difference in comfort. My backside can finally breathe. The idea of not wearing the running belt potentially helping the chafing is encouraging. I loop the belt around my backpack to keep it off me.

Eventually, the sweat dripping off my backpack slows to nearly nothing. I'm not sure if it's the shade from all the trees since I'm back in the forest, the fact that the sun is going down, or that I'm not wearing the waist belt anymore—but I'm beginning to feel better. I'm still walking the chafed waddle of wet shorts, and the friction on my lower back is getting worse, but everything else is better than it was. *Progress.*

I roll up my microfiber towel and wedge it between my back and backpack, where the chafing is taking place. It's an instant winner. Immediate relief. My back gets a little airflow since the majority of my bag is off my spine now. The towel seems to be collecting any other excess sweat coming down, keeping my rear end a little less wet. I shove my spare socks under my shoulder straps to keep them from rubbing my shoulders raw, too.

The only piece of clothing I'm wearing now is a pair of two-inch running shorts with slits all the way up to the waistband. It's basically a loincloth with booty coverage. And that is now the only part of my body that's wet and uncomfortable. Uncomfortable is an understatement. My thighs are all but bleeding at this point. I can only imagine what someone would be thinking if they saw me right now. Socks on my shoulders under my shoulder straps, nothing but shoes and a loincloth, walking like a penguin. I mean… what a sight.

Thankfully, I haven't seen anyone on the trail since I left the Bogachiel River trailhead. The rainforest is humid. The air is thick. Even though the sun has gone down and I'm not sweating nearly as much, my shorts aren't getting any drier. *I have to get my shorts dry if I want a successful day tomorrow.*

Screw it.

I take my shorts off.

The only things on me at this point are my backpack and shoes. (And my shoulder socks. Let's not forget about my shoulder socks.)

Again, instant relief. Praise the Lord for airflow and the absence of wet clothing. *We were born naked for a reason.*

It's past 9:00 p.m. now, and I'm nowhere near where I wanted to get to for the night. I'm only on mile 37. My pace while maintaining this waddle walk is horrendous. *I'm getting at least 40 trail miles before I stop. I can't have a sub-40-mile day out here.* (And no, my 1.3 miles one way in the wrong direction doesn't count toward the 40.)

I'd prefer to get at least 45, but I also know I shouldn't overdo my "time on feet," especially in the beginning of this journey. Joe McConaughy insisted several times before I started that I need to keep my "time on feet" to 13–14 hours a day max for the first week or two until my body gets used to the mileage. I already hiked over 16 hours yesterday. And I'm nearing 16 hours for today too. Granted, I did stop at Bogachiel State Park for a couple of hours. *I guess today is really only about 14 hours ON my feet. I'll stop at 40 miles.*

As I approach the camp area I'm sleeping at tonight, I come upon a stream. I stop and stare at the cold, flowing water, then sit down in it. It's not very deep, but it's soothing. I splash the water on myself, trying to wash my lower half off. It's bitter cold, refreshing, and clean. Did I mention clean?

When I reach the campsite, I don't see signs of other campers. *Score. I get this whole place to myself.* I lay out my bivy, a human-sized sack with a waterproof bottom and a breathable top designed for ultralight hikers to sleep in, in lieu of a tent. I like to pitch a tarp over mine if it's going to rain. If conditions are ideal, I won't even get inside; I'll just sleep on top of it. And that's what tonight is—ideal conditions. I lie down and look up; there's not a cloud in the sky. I'm sleeping under the stars tonight.

HIKING IN THE BUFF

THE NEXT MORNING I decide my primary goal should be reducing, or preferably eliminating, the chafing. *I have to get this under control.* I take a close look at the damage, to see if there's any progress from last night. *Ouch. That's going to scar.*

My clothes are back on. It's dark and chilly out. The sun should be up soon. The trail tread is forgiving. Soft under my feet. The trails are clean, freshly maintained. *Don't get used to it, Nick.* I knew coming into this hike that Olympic National Park would likely have the cleanest trails. I'm expecting lots of overgrowth once I get past the peninsula. I've already met a few hikers who warned, "There are 1,200 blowdowns in the Pasayten. And no, that's not a hyperbole," and "I hiked through 20 miles of blowdowns in the Pasayten." *Don't get used to it, Nick. Don't get used to it.*

The trees get bigger and bigger the farther up the Bogachiel River I climb. The forests of Olympic National Park are really something else. Something every person should get to experience at some point in their life. There's an aura in these forests that's hard to explain. It's lush and fresh, with a scent of musty decaying wood mixed with pure oxygen. It's proof the earth is alive. The trees aren't as tall as redwoods and not nearly as fat as sequoias, but aside from those two species in California, I've never seen a bigger tree outside of Olympic National Park. The Olympic Peninsula has some of the largest cedar, spruce, and fir trees in the world. Although I am surprised the PNT travels up alongside the Bogachiel and not the Hoh River. The Hoh Rainforest seems to have bigger trees, and it even parallels the Bogachiel, so it logistically works with the direction of the trail too. *Fewer people are on the Bogachiel, though; maybe that's why.*

Shortly into the climb up toward Low Divide, I start sweating. It's not that hot out, but the humidity of the rainforest is dense. In an effort to prevent my shorts from getting soaking wet again, and since I haven't seen anyone on this trail since the trailhead, I'm back to hiking naked in the wilderness. My inner thighs are still raw. I'm still walking the waddle walk. *Can't afford any more casualties down there.*

Mmmmm. Huckleberries. I'm getting distracted easily. The berries are everywhere, thick and plump. I try to master the "drive-by" huckleberry picking, but my pace says, "No." I laugh at myself. Imagine some guy frolicking through the forest without any shorts on. He quickly snatches a couple of berries off each bush as he wobbles by and tosses them in his mouth in one fluid movement. Berries on the go. It's a swift waddle berry graze.

Four hours later, I'm up on a ridgeline headed toward Bogachiel Peak. All of a sudden, I see a couple near their 50s walking in my direction. I scuffle back a few steps and jump off the trail behind some bushes to put my shorts back on. *Did they see me?! Maybe the huckleberry bushes alongside the trail were tall enough.* The bushes were about waist-high after all. I get back on the trail and continue in their direction. We make eye contact. The lady begins to giggle. *Yeah… They saw me.*

"These huckleberries are delicious." I try to play it off.

"I'm sure they are," they grin. "There's a bear up ahead on the other side of that hill munching on some if you want to join it."

I do want to join it. My walk increases to a soft prance. Imagine the Grinch, creeping through Who Village, hunched over with a smirk of mischief. I need to get over that hill before the bear is gone, but I don't want to scare it off either.

Hours go by, but I never see the bear they mentioned. I make it over another mountain pass and head back downhill. I stop to do my business off the trail a little ways and find a log to set my bag, hat, and glasses on while I dig a hole. A half-mile later down the hill, I realize I forgot my glasses. They are wood-grain glasses. They blend in with leaves, wood, and the ground. They can be tough to find if they drop off something. *They must have fallen off the log. I must have thought they were in a pocket somewhere.*

I still have my prescription sunglasses. Do I *really* need my regular glasses? *Yes. Yes, I do.* I'm not completely blind without them, but with how much traveling I'm doing in the dark—and with it being so early in the hike—I really do need my glasses. Besides that, for me to truly appreciate the beauty of this hike, I want to see in 4k. Without my glasses, it's only 360p. And 360p is a disservice to the mountains.

I run back uphill, trying to minimize the time lost by backtracking. *Bam! There they are.* Right beside the log on the ground. On they go, and I'm double-timing back down the mountain. Down into a valley and then back uphill again. It's time to cross another pass.

By the time I make it to Appleton Pass, the sun is beginning to set. I still have a ways to go. *It's all downhill from here till I make camp, though.* On the way down the mountain, it begins to get dark. The trail becomes overgrown. *I guess nobody hikes this side of Appleton Pass very often.* All of a sudden, I hear a sound just a short distance up ahead. It's an animal. A large animal.

It's too dark to see very far, but I know that sound. Different animals have different sounds, and after you've spent enough time in the wilderness, you learn the difference between those sounds. Large hoofed animals like moose and elk make a similar noise as they walk. Deer are swifter and lighter. Cougars are nearly silent. But bears… bears make a very distinct sound with the way they walk. They are foragers. They claw at the ground to dig up food. They crush rotting logs and turn them over to get what's inside. They huff and they puff. They grunt.

It's definitely a bear up ahead. I'm frankly a little surprised I'm just now getting close to one today. I've seen bear scat on the trails all day long, and huckleberry bushes have been stripped clean while enough bushes were still ripe for the picking—enough to keep the bears around.

I hear it suddenly scurry off into the woods. *It must have seen, heard, or smelled me.*

By 10:00 p.m. I'm nearing the Olympic Hot Springs. They aren't marked on my map, but I notice from all the comments on Guthooks that there are thermal pools you can soak in.

For the next three miles, I can't stop thinking about how good it would feel to bathe in warm water. *I'll stop for just 10 minutes. It'll do my legs, and probably even my raw skin, some good.* As I near the area, I discover that to get to them, you have to go downhill off the main trail, across a bridge to the other side of a sizable mountain stream, and back uphill on the other side. *You mean I have to lose time by going out of the way to get to where I was going to lose time by soaking? How bad do I want that soak?* But I've already made up my mind. I'm getting some hot tub action tonight. And so out of the way I go.

Look at me. Am I trying to set an FKT, or am I just thru-hiking? If it's not starfish, it's arches and keyholes to explore. If it's not that, it's the huckleberries. Now I'm headed to a hot tub from Mother Nature? I need to stop getting distracted.

After I cross the bridge, I see a shallow stream of sulfur water only twelve inches wide. The smell reminds me of Yellowstone. I'm tired and frustrated that the hot spring pool is so far out of the way. I can only see as far as my headlamp allows. I've been using the waddle walk of shame all day long to protect my raw-chafed thighs, so my pace has been terrible. I follow the stream, hoping the pool is only seconds away. But it doesn't appear. *Screw the full immersion leg soak. I'm here. There's sulfur water. Surely it'll have some kind of healing properties in it for my skin.*

There's a flat spot about 25 feet away. I lay my gear down and strip. Then, sit down in the rank and splash the warm water over my body. It's soothing. Who cares what it smells like? I stink anyway. Within a couple of minutes, I decide it's enough. The longer I sit here, the harder it'll be to get up. The water isn't even deep enough to soak in. I need to get going, and I need to get to sleep. *Ha! If I could only do both of those at the same time.*

I walk back over to my gear and gaze upon the small, flat spot. It's the perfect size for a one-person tent. I can hear the mountain stream down below. The stars are out. I just washed off my raw skin. *I could sleep really well here tonight and give my thighs a chance to heal.*

As I'm lying down, looking up at the stars, I can still smell sulfur. I think back and wonder. *What if that hot spring pool is just another 50 feet up the hill? Forget it. You're already lying down. Just go to sleep.*

THE CUTTING OF THE SLEEVES

A LIGHT RAIN WAKES ME. It's barely past 2:00 a.m. I rush to set up my tarp. *You're in a rainforest; why didn't you just pitch the tarp last night regardless of the clear sky and stars?*

Just a few hours later, I'm back on my feet. The sprinkling has ceased, but it's still overcast and significantly cooler out. I'm back to running. Oh, how it feels good to be making good time again. The inner thigh chafing isn't too bad, and my right ankle seems to have loosened back up; it was bugging me quite a bit yesterday. *Maybe that hot spring was a good idea after all. Or maybe it was the sleep.*

Yesterday, for whatever reason, my right ankle had a sharp pain in it when I would run or walk normally, but if I added this gangster swag step where I bent my right foot inward and didn't step too far back with it—only letting my left leg do a full swing—it alleviated most of the discomfort. One might also describe it as a swift zombie walk. *Nah, I'm not dirty or scraggly enough to be a zombie yet. It's only been four days.*

By afternoon, I'm climbing another ascent. It's warming up despite the clouds blocking out the sun. I can feel the chafing acting up underneath my arms again. If I hold my arms up so the wet sleeves don't rub on my sides, it seems to prevent the irritation. *I'm so glad there aren't many people on this trail.* I chuckle at myself. *I would be the laughingstock of every hiker group. "Hey, did you all see that guy walking for miles with his hands out in the air like he was flying?" "What was with his zombie walk anyway?" "Yeah, he kinda stunk like sulfur too."*

My arms are tired. I keep rotating between holding my arms out like a buff bodybuilder who can't lay his arms down on his sides and resting my hands on my head. If I take my shirt off, it'll help the chafing below my armpits, but then my shoulders would get raw from my backpack straps. *I could cut the sleeves off.* I really don't want to do that. This is my favorite shirt.

A few switchbacks later, I'm pulling out my UL pocket knife, my razor blade. It makes quick work of the sleeves. It's another instant winner. It's dumping heat, and airflow has increased. *Why didn't I do this sooner?* (UL stands for ultralight, but most ultralight hikers want to shave the weight off of those extra letters, so they whittle it down to just UL.)

As I make it to the top of the climb, a light, drizzly rain begins. I can see it completely pouring in the valley I just came from. *Good timing, I suppose.* A cold breeze comes in to chill the air off even more. The cooler temperatures are bolstering quicker movement. I'm feeling strong again, and the chafing is proving to be manageable with the adjustments I've made. *Ha! Within four days, I've vowed to never wear underwear again, cut the sleeves off my shirt, wedged a rolled-up towel between my backpack and back, and mastered the waddle walk so well I can do it while running.*

People! I see people! Several groups of hikers are up ahead, all bundled up in rain gear from head to toe. Some could even pass for wearing full-out winter gear. I'm in my shorty shorts, newly made sleeveless shirt, and wearing a backpack small enough that most people think it's a day hiker's bag. I jog toward a couple of backpackers who look like they've been on the trail much longer than a weekend getaway. They are a little dirtier, a little more worn, and they have the look of experience. Their gear is more accessible. Water bottles are in shoulder pockets. A few items hang from their sternum straps. They have fanny packs. *PNT hikers.*

I point to them and ask, "PNT?"

They raise their trekking poles to point west and respond back, "Yeah, we're headed to the coast now. What about you?"

"Me too! I just left the coast. You're going to love it."

"Wait, you're on the PNT?"

"Yeah."

"Your bag looks so small."

"Your bag looks heavy."

They laugh. "When did you start?"

"Monday."

"Monday?! You started on Monday?!" (It's currently Thursday.) They've stopped and turned around to face me at this point since we've passed each other.

"Yeah."

"That's gotta be more than 40 miles a day."

"Forty-nine the first day, but I've slowed down since then."

They stare at me in disbelief as I keep jogging away.

"Enjoy your hike!" I shout, as we're getting too far away from each other to keep the conversation going.

I pass by a few more hikers. It feels awkward with everyone staring at me. *Is it because I'm running, or is it because I'm wearing so little clothing compared to everyone else in this chilly, drizzly rain?*

One guy cheers, "Hell yeah! Get some!" He gives me a high five as I run past him.

Soon the trails are vacant, and I'm back in solitude. The rain has stopped. The clouds are dropping so low it's becoming a patchy fog. I see a sharply defined rainbow. Wait, no, it's a double rainbow. The one below it is just harder to see, and it's getting harder to see the thicker the fog becomes. *I'm running through clouds and rainbows. Freaking awesome.*

As I near the national park boundary, I approach a couple of park employees, a guy and a gal. One yells from about 50 feet away to get my attention, "That's a mighty small pack you have there."

"The smaller the pack, the faster and farther you can go," I reply.

"Where you headed?" the man asks.

"Montana."

"Montana?!"

"Yeah, Montana. I'm hiking the Pacific Northwest Trail."

The gal chimes in, "That's from the coast all the way to Glacier National Park, right?"

"You've got it!"

She asks, "When did you leave the coast?"

"Monday."

The guy quibbles, "No, you didn't."

"Yeah, I did." *Are we about to have an arguing match out here?* I giggle inside.

He contends, "You left the coast near Port Angeles and came up here from the north."

"I started at Cape Alava and went down the coast to the Hoh River before cutting back to cross the Olympics."

He still doesn't believe me. "That's impossible. That's gotta be 200 miles."

"Not quite 200 miles, but I have been doing 40 or so miles a day. I did 49 the first day, but I've slowed down since then. Well, I guess today is looking like it could be a 50-mile day."

"You *slowed down* to 40 miles a day," he chuckles.

The girl chimes in again, "What kind of shoes are you wearing?"

"Altra Lone Peaks."

"I run ultras here and there, is why I was asking. I've been curious to try those. It's always fun to meet other ultrarunners on the trail," she remarks.

Ultrarunner. That term has always fascinated me. She's an ultrarunner. But she mentioned "meeting other ultrarunners on the trail." Is she saying I'm an ultrarunner? I'm not an ultrarunner. Wait... I do run more than a marathon. And I guess an ultra is anything more than a marathon. But I've never technically been in an "ultra race." I've never thought of myself as an ultrarunner before. Heck, I didn't even know what an ultra was eight months ago.

"I went through four different kinds of trail runners last year, and once I found these, I was hooked. They are so comfy. OK, I've got to get going. You guys have a good night!"

I've been running the majority of the day, and my legs feel great. The temperatures have been amazing. I've been getting confidence boosters all day long with the comments people have been dishing out. *Today has been fun.* I make it out the other side of Olympic National Park. It feels good to cross the entire park, including the length of the coast, in four days. *Would've been cooler if it were three days.*

CAMPING ON A BLUFF

I'M UP AT 4:00 A.M., moving by 4:20. I need to push to make it to Port Townsend for my resupply box and to catch a ferry across the Puget Sound. A mouse was at the campsite last night. It came out around 1:00 a.m. and persisted to annoy me the rest of the night. I didn't get the best sleep. *Maybe I'll stay away from heavily camped areas and just focus on flat ground from now on.*

It's mostly a downhill, easy cruise on dirt roads coming out of the Olympics into Port Townsend. I feel like I'm flying. My watch dings to tell me I've reached my 30,000-step goal for the day. I've never set a "step goal" on my watch before. I don't even know how to change those settings. Whatever factory setting my watch has that automatically adjusts itself based on your daily average is apparently capped at a goal limit of 30,000 steps. I giggle and smile. *It's only 7:30; the sun is barely even up.* I feel like I'm starting to get the hang of this FKT thing.

Despite my mental confidence, I physically ache. The top of my left foot hurts. That ankle feels weak. At least my right ankle isn't bothering me anymore, and at least the foot pain isn't in the exact spot I fractured back in April. *Something different hurts every day—and I'm just getting started.*

I stop and take off my shoes to address a hot spot. Dirt is collecting between my pinky toes; it's in the early stages of rubbing one of them raw. I clean the grime out from between my piggies, apply some ointment, and wiggle on my toe socks. *Thank goodness Joe told me to watch out for that pinky toe dirt and to bring toe socks; that could have been my first blister.* One of my heels is beginning to look a little raw now, too. *Better go ahead and put some Leuko tape on that while I'm at it.*

Keep moving.

A few miles later, I realize I've lost the microfiber towel I had wedged between my back and backpack to help with the lower back chafing. *Shoot. At least I'll be in Port Townsend soon. I'll buy another one at the grocery store on my way through.*

I step off-trail to answer nature's call. About a minute later, as I'm navigating through the brush, I feel a sharp burning sensation on my leg. *Did something in that bush just bite me?* I smack my leg and keep moving.

All of a sudden, my leg brushes up against another plant. It burns. It stings. As I'm leaning over to look at it, my other leg gets bitten by another one of these weeds. *Ahhhh! It's on fire!!* Rashes instantly welt up on my legs where they had minor contact with this poisonous devil. *What the hell is this thing?* I take pictures to document. It has tiny needles all along its stalk. It makes you itch just by looking at it. It's everywhere. How did I get so far back in this mess? Is this some hardcore version of poison ivy? I'm horribly allergic to poison ivy.

Thank goodness I brought the calf gaiters. I carefully put them on while trying my best not to touch any more of the irritant. I'm not careful enough, though, because my right butt cheek rubs up against Mr. Devil Plant in the process. *Cheeks of fire!* (Yes, I was wearing shorts in this moment; they're just really short shorts. Get your mind out of the gutter.)

It's far too warm for extra layers right now, but my rain jacket goes on. It's my shell of protection against the tiny needles of this awful cluster. I pull the hood over my head tight and hunker down like a bulldozer. I weave and skate my way back—trying to only let my rain jacket, calf gaiters, or shoes touch the gates of hell.

The forest service road is so overgrown, you'd never even know it was originally designed for cars. Bushes and trees are growing in the middle of it. It's a powerful reminder of how quickly the earth can take something back. You'd be hard-pressed to even call it a trail. I joke with myself. *Do you see a trail? Because I don't see a trail.*

A few hours later, I get cell service and post the photos of the awful stinging plant on Facebook. One of my friends who lives in Washington types, "Hey, so something helpful I should have thought of, we have stinging nettle here." So thanks, Josh. Thanks for telling me about the stinging nettle AFTER I discovered it on my own.

Soon I'm running the shoulders, and sometimes nonexistent shoulders, of a two-lane highway into Port Townsend. I'd move farther off to the side if it were possible, but in some places, it's a high drop-off cliff on the other side of the guardrail. I'm forced to be on this narrow shoulder between the guardrail and the road. Cars zoom by within a couple of feet of me. The wind from a box truck tries to knock the hat off my head, but I hold on to it with one hand while bracing myself on the guardrail with the other. Sketchy.

Once I'm off the narrow highway and going through the small city of Port Townsend, I'm able to appreciate how many blackberries there are. They've been covering the fences nearly the entire way here. I occasionally grab a few berries and eat them on the go, being cautious not to stop for too many. *I can't miss my resupply box or the ferry.*

A scraggly-looking fellow with a long, untamed beard riding a bicycle loaded down with random assortments is riding in my direction. As I'm running toward him and he's riding toward me, he offers, "Want to share a mint with me?" "Sure," I respond—not really knowing what's going to happen. He hands me a green peppermint sealed in a wrapper and shouts, "God bless!" as he rides off. *How random is that?* I inspect the peppermint wrapper. It hasn't been tampered with. This isn't some candy creep conspiracy. This is just a nice man, who very well could have all his belongings with him, riding his bike and sharing his afternoon joy: some mints. *I never would have guessed a bearded man giving me a mint while riding a bicycle would have been one of my highlights out here.*

I'm off the streets and onto a city bike path for the next few miles. It's nice not having to deal with traffic. I come up to a couple of people unloading bikes from their car. They look at me with excited eyes. "You are moving quick! We passed you on the highway as we were driving in. Where are you headed?"

"Montana. I'm on the Pacific Northwest Trail."

"How cool! How many miles is that?"

"1,248. I'm nearly one-fifth of the way through it!"

"Wow. We are only biking 15 miles today, out and back. Maybe we will see you on our way back to the car."

A couple of miles later, I see a runner get on the trail in front of me. *Think I can catch 'em?* I'm on mile 38 for the day. *He might be a little fresher than me, probably going faster.* Within 10 minutes, the runner is completely out of my vision and has left me in the dust. *Yup, definitely faster.*

OK, but seriously, someone planted all these blackberries to try and slow me down. *Freaking delicious.* Blackberries are one of my favorite fruits. And these are some good friggin' berries. Or maybe I'm just happy to have something fresh and juicy instead of prepackaged foods that have been squished into Ziplocs and used as a pillow for a few nights.

I see the masts and stowed sails of sailboats up ahead. I've made it to the marina. *The Safeway should be just around that corner.* I scurry past the docks and through the gate to the other side. *Oh, it's closer than I thought it'd be. I just have to cross the street.*

As I'm walking through the Safeway parking lot, in the handicapped parking spots near the front of the store, I see a pig. It's a light beige color with big dark spots and a curly yet surprisingly hairy tail. It's on a pink leash with a pink harness. "Ummm. Can I take a picture of your pig? I'm sorry. I've just never seen a pig at the grocery store before." *Not a live pig anyway.* She laughs, "Of course." Someone else is already taking a picture of it. I think she's used to the celebrity status.

I'm in and out as quickly as possible. Shopping doesn't take long, but the checkout lines are awful. *How is every checkout line backed up into the aisles?* No microfiber towel or at least that's what an employee tells me—I'm not taking the time to search for one—but I have more ibuprofen, Aquaphor, and a gallon of lemonade now.

I'm walking through the parking lot, headed back toward the route through Port Townsend. I'll pick up my resupply box next. As I'm adjusting my bag and waist belt, I drop the lemonade. The plastic bottle busts open. It shatters instantly upon impact with the pavement. It spills everywhere.

"I saw that! I saw that!" yells an employee collecting shopping carts.

"Man…" *I was really looking forward to that lemonade.*

"Go get another one. I saw it happen. Just tell them it broke before you left the property line, and you can get a new one for free."

"Really? Wow. Thank you. You're my favorite person in the world right now. I love you. Thank you so much."

I toss the broken jug in the trash on the way in the store, and I'm back out with a new one a couple of minutes later. No time to wait in line at customer service, mess with a return, process receipts and everything. That'd take too long. This employee just gave me permission to get a replacement. So I'm doing just that. In and out with a new gallon of lemonade, skipping any form of check-out line. I feel guilty yet empowered with my newfound permission to get another lemonade for free.

OK. No more delays.

No other customers are at the UPS store. *Thank you.* This should be quick. I ask the lady handing me my box if she knows anything about the ferry. "They are real strict on time. You have to get there early to make sure you get on." *I'll go through my box and repack my bag on the ferry.* I finish crossing Port Townsend—sometimes balancing the box on my head, sometimes carrying it like a football—and buy my ferry ticket. I sit down outside the terminal. "When is the next one supposed to load?" Someone replies, "In less than 10 minutes." *Perfect timing. I can take a break now.* I'm ahead of schedule. Several hours ahead of when I thought I'd be here. I'm making great time. *You should be. You've been running all day long.*

The ferry ride goes by quicker than I expect. I barely have time to plug in my devices and repack my bag from the resupply box. I originally envisioned myself on the top deck of the ferry, leaning on the railing, looking out over the open waters—but instead I'm being ushered off the boat by a ferry worker before I've even been able to throw my trash away.

The sun is still up. My original game plan was to camp at the state park right here, where you get off the ferry, but the campground is full. There's nowhere else to legally camp here. I look at the time and check my map. *I could make it another 10 miles.* Guthooks indicates the next beach walk along the Puget Sound requires low tide, and it just so happens to be low tide right now.

On the way to the beach, I find a campground bathroom with electricity. I can spare 30 minutes; this next tide section isn't too long. *I'd better take this opportunity to top off my electronics.* I scarf down a bunch of the extra food stuffed in my bag from my resupply. My bag is heavy again; getting rid of weight and throwing away as much trash as possible is my focus while I let my devices charge for half an hour. I meet a guy camped near the bathroom who's been bicycling across the U.S. for the last year. He's already been from coast to coast and is now back up in Washington before heading toward Arizona. His story is captivating. It makes me want to hear more, but it's time to go.

As I approach the beach, I see an old fort bunker built into the ground. *Ugh, man, not fair. I don't really have time to explore all this… but I NEED to explore all this.* I run down the concrete stairs into the stronghold. Names are written all over the walls. Railing runs through the center, showing where a cannon used to be mounted. The view from the far end is postcard-worthy. The sun is getting close to setting over the Puget Sound. The beach, the waves, the mountains in the background. *Definitely worth the detour.* I stare at the ocean just a little while longer. *OK, gotta go.*

By the time I'm on sand, I'm checking my live tracker page, one of the requirements for FKT verification, and it turns out my Garmin InReach hasn't been reporting my coordinates every 30 minutes like it should. Big gaps are in my tracking. *Was the signal blocked by the dense forests of Olympic National Park? Did I accidentally turn the tracking off when I locked the screen in an attempt to preserve battery?* I'm freaking out. *Is everything I just did for nothing?* I'm blowing up Joe's phone texting him if this is a problem or not. He's not responding. *This is an emergency!!*

I call Hannah, and she calms me down by reminding me of some of the FKT verification rules. I have plenty of pictures to prove coordinates where there's a gap in tracking, and I've been taking detailed trail notes. Everything should be fine, but I still feel incredibly uneasy about it. *Why am I crying?* My emotions are all out of whack. *I'm probably just tired.*

The trail climbs up a bluff on Whidbey Island. The last bits of the sunset are fading away. A cruise ship is headed off to sea. I can see the Olympic Mountains behind the sound, towering in the background like a big brother watching over the waters. The very peaks of the Olympics are covered by clouds; it's quiet and calming. I wish Hannah were here with me to enjoy this moment.

I check the map and mileage. I've gone 49.5 miles today. I keep scratching just below that 50-mile mark. *I can go 49.5, but I can't go 50?* It's as if my subconscious is saying, "Nope. You're not ready for 50 miles yet." I haven't necessarily been pushing for 50-mile days. In fact, I should be doing low mileage until my body gets used to this; it just keeps working out this way. Sometimes your mileage is dictated by where you can sleep.

It's day five, and I'm at mile 238.3 on the map. I've already been on my feet for 16 hours. *I should stop.* I lie down on my bivy in the only flat spot on top of the cliff. It's not perfectly level, but it'll do. I position my body so my feet are uphill. I'd rather my feet be elevated anyway. My legs are instantly grateful, so happy. My feet are throbbing. They hurt so bad, but they feel so good to be done for the day at the same time. It's a subtle euphoria. Somehow I enjoy it.

There's no rain forecasted, and the skies are clear, so I don't even bother setting up my tarp. I'm cowboy camping tonight. *Who wouldn't want to cowboy camp on top of a bluff overlooking the Puget Sound and Olympic Mountains anyway?*

I go through my nightly foot massage and "doctor the nether regions" routine while I think about the day. *Wow. I haven't been limping on my left foot for nearly 15 miles.* It's as if I had an epiphany: "If you're hurting, just keep running, and eventually everything will work itself out," signed, the Worst Advice Ever.

BEATEN TO DEATH

IT WAS HARD TO FALL ASLEEP last night; my feet were splitting with pain. I need to take it easy for the next few days to make sure my body stays healthy for the long haul. I have to stop doing these 16-hour days so early in the trip. *I'll sleep in today to force myself to have fewer hours on my feet.* It doesn't take me long to push my alarm back to 6:30 a.m.

But before my alarm goes off, I wake up to a wet quilt. A thick coastal fog has rolled in. I quickly pitch my tarp to shield from any more moisture soaking into my gear, but it's mostly too late. *You should have known that, Nick. Should have put the tarp up being near all this cold ocean water.* I'll have to dry my quilt out later in the sun. *Would the tarp have even helped? Would the fog have rolled in under my tarp anyway?*

The morning starts off mystical. I'm walking through clouds. The sandy trail parallels the ocean. I know there's a cliff straight down to the beach on the left and a small forest on my right, but with this hazy shroud, I can't see the cliff, much less the water down below. It's just a wall of white. I can barely even see the trees a few feet away from me at times.

I take my phone off airplane mode. Joe has messaged me back. He confirms what Hannah told me the previous night about my tracker not saving my coordinates like it should. "It's not great, but you have photos to prove coordinates, worst-case scenario. Don't worry about the tracker."

Phew! What a relief. I tell him I made it 49 miles yesterday.

He replies, "49.5 miles? That's killer. How much time have you been spending on your feet?"

Crap. I'm busted.

Joe was adamant that I limit my time on feet in the beginning of this journey, and here I am telling on myself. But in reality, I didn't have much of a choice. Day one I was racing the tides. Last night, I was rushing to catch the ferry. Then the campground on the other side of the ferry was full... I'm trying to justify my actions.

The trail zigs and zags its way down to the beach. A sea otter runs across the sand in front of me, from behind a pile of driftwood by the cliffs, all the way to the water—he dives in without making a splash. From driftwood to gone within seconds.

I come across a portion of the beach that's clearly underwater during high tide, only passable during low tide. The water lines go a few feet up the cliff. *I completely forgot to check the tides for this section.* I check the charts. It's the peak of low tide. *How convenient. I don't even try to time this one right, and it works out perfectly anyway.*

Miles later, I'm off the beach and following the paved roads of the island. I find a microfiber towel on the shoulder within minutes. *Manna from heaven!* I shake it off and smell it. It doesn't even stink. *Score.* I roll it up and wedge it between my back and backpack.

Soon, I find myself walking out of a hole-in-the-wall gas station with a couple of Dr Peppers in my hand. I sit down in the shade of the building to take my shoes off and inspect my feet. A guy in a truck drives up, stops with his window rolled down, and asks, "Do you need anything?"

I probably look homeless. "No, I'm good, thanks. I'm just hiking."

"I know," he replies, "but I didn't know if you might need something like some water or a couple of bucks."

This guy is just trying to give me some trail magic. "Thank you, really, thank you—but I'm good. I don't need anything right now."

Trail magic is typically referred to as any act of generosity given to a thru-hiker in need by a trail angel. It could be food, a shower, laundry, or even a ride to or from a resupply town. A trail angel is any person who helps a thru-hiker out of the goodness in their heart.

A few more people stop and offer to help me throughout the day. I still don't need anything, so I decline their offers, but it's nice to know there are so many kind people in the world.

These roads are killing my feet. When I originally looked at the map, I figured this part would be easy. No elevation gain. No obstacles. Just flats. *Surely that's where I'll make up a ton of ground.* But no. The asphalt and concrete are wearing on me. I miss the soft, forgiving grounds of the Washington foot trails. My feet are being beaten to death.

It's much safer to walk on the left side of the road, to be able to see the oncoming traffic in front of you. But I find myself moving from one side to the other, testing the grounds to see which has a softer shoulder for my feet. Sometimes it helps. Sometimes it doesn't. *At least there's not much traffic out here.*

I walk past a golf course and overhear someone on the green talking to his golf buddy, "Hey look, there's a long-haired hippie dude."

Four fighter jets fly over me, all lined up in unison. *No barrel rolls like they did in Death Valley this past winter, though.*

More blackberries.

It's hot. I check the weather. *How is it this hot when it's only 79 degrees?* Maybe it's the sun reflecting off the black asphalt. Maybe it's the absolute absence of shade on these roads. Maybe this weather app is lying to me. Maybe I'm just a baby in the heat. *This isn't even heat, Nick.* I'm thankful it isn't 100 degrees. I ran into a PNT hiker a couple of days ago who revealed his shoes melted on the asphalt during a 115-degree day this summer.

As I'm checking comments on Guthooks, I get excited by the fact that there are a couple of trail angels up ahead who live directly on the trail. Technically, this portion of the PNT is a road, but nevertheless, it's the trail. Notes advise they'll let you camp in their yard, fill your water, and charge your devices.

As I'm walking up to their house, a dog starts barking at me. I hesitate. And then I hear a voice, "There must be a thru-hiker. Come on in here." An older, shorter gentleman walks up to me, asks what I need, and begins ushering me inside his house with the warmest of welcomes.

"Some water, and maybe if I could charge some of my devices?"

He offers, "How about some apples and peaches too? Oh! I might still have some homemade peach muffins!" He proceeds to tell me about some of his and his wife's hiking adventures. His wife is currently hiking the Wonderland Trail around Mount Rainier. He is going through chemo right now, so he wasn't able to go on the trip with her, but he didn't want her to miss out on a once-in-a-lifetime opportunity, so he sent her on ahead. It can be difficult to get a permit for the Wonderland Trail—I know—I've tried to get one before.

He's full of energy and excitement. His stories are fascinating. His generosity is endless. I can tell this isn't going to be a fast stop; I don't want to be rude and cut him off short, so I just accept the fact that this will be at least an hour-long break in the day. He continues to share some of their hiking tales and explains why he likes being a trail angel so much. He's literally offered me anything you can think of, except a shower. So I slip it in, "Is there any possible chance I could take a shower?"

"Of course! Here, let me show you…" He takes me to their bathroom and brings me a fresh, clean towel.

Warm, running water. And cleanliness. This is the farthest, by far, I've ever hiked without a shower before. It's tempting to forget about time. I dry my head with the towel and talk to myself in the mirror. *But don't get used to it, Nick. You've still got another 1,000 miles to go.*

When I come back into the kitchen, he greets me with a paper sack full of homemade peach muffins, two apples, and a peach. "These are all from our yard, fresh from this morning. Now get going. I know you said you're on a time crunch."

"I can't thank you enough!" I reply after he walks me outside and back to the road.

Just a few miles later, my feet are thankful to be back on actual foot trails at Deception Pass. *There's a PNT marker!* First PNT emblem I've seen on the trail, and I'm 260 miles in. My feet are butchered. My arches are destroyed. My pace has been pitiful. Now that I'm back on softer ground, my spirits are lifted, and I'm beginning to move faster. Or so I thought. All of a sudden, a runner passes me. *What the hell? How am I getting passed right now? I never get passed. I'm the one supposed to be doing the passing.* I keep telling myself I'm on mile 30 for the day, and he's probably only on mile one.

I cross the iconic bridge that Deception Pass is known for. I'm reminded of when Hannah and I came through here in our Volkswagen Vanagon a couple of years ago. The roads are narrow and winding, with limited parking and bumper-to-bumper traffic. *Ha! I'm moving faster on foot than we did in the van.* I'm holding on to anything that makes me feel faster since I was just passed up by a runner.

I come across a cave. It looks like a mine. *Just keep moving, Nick.* I've always been fascinated by caves, tunnels, and mines and such. It's like a magnet, luring me in. The trail goes north. I go west into the cave. *I'll just explore it for two minutes. In and out.* And here I am again, taking detours of exploration while I'm supposed to be setting an FKT. By the way, it's never "just two minutes."

A small store appears. Big red letters read, "LAKE ERIE GROCERY." *Why didn't I know about this? I could have carried less food and bought more here.* I walk inside and realize it's more of a convenience store than a grocery store. It doesn't take me long to grab a few snacks and a lemonade—but my feet are pulsating. I can barely stand to remain standing. As I approach the counter to check out, I awkwardly ask the clerk, "Ummm. I'm sorry, but my feet hurt really, really, really bad. Is it OK if I kneel down?" Before she can respond, I get down on my knees while explaining how many miles I've hiked. "And is there a place in here I could refill my water bottle?" I sound desperate. I am desperate. This poor pitiful human, begging on his knees for water.

She looks down at me, then looks at the food I'm already buying on the counter. I grab a handful of Jolly Ranchers in the bucket next to the cash register and dump them on the counter. "These too."

"Give me your water bottle. There's nowhere in the store to refill it, but I live out back. This is my family's store. I'll go fill it up in my kitchen."

"Thank you so much!"

Afterward, I'm walking through the ACFL (Anacortes Community Forest Land). The sun is getting close to setting, and there's no camping allowed out here. I check the map—after the ACFL, I'll be walking through a town, an industrial complex, and then more town roads for what seems like well over 30 miles. *Where the hell am I supposed to camp?* Just keep moving.

Just before the sun goes down, I stop for a break on a footbridge. My feet ache like I've never felt before. They are pounding—it's taking over my mind. *Is it the hard asphalt, or is it my shoes? Are they supposed to hurt this bad?* I'm still in a "no camping" zone, and I'm about to be in a "there's no way I'll get away with that" camping zone (aka the town of Anacortes). *After 9:30, I'll just stop at the next flat spot I see.* I look at my mileage. *I'm on flat ground, and I've only moved 32 miles?* It's defeating. I know I need to take it easy since I've started off with so many long-hour and high-mileage days, but only 32? *Don't stop until you have 35.*

By 10:00 p.m. I'm lying down on top of my bivy in the middle of the trail. It's the only doable flat spot I've seen for hours. Not wide enough for a tent, but a bivy—a bivy is the perfect size. The stars are out, I'm not next to cold ocean water to potentially cause fog, and the weather app indicates it's a clear night. I go through my nightly routine, spending a little extra time on my feet, and get ready for some more cowboy camping.

THE LIFESTYLE CHANGE OF A FARMER'S TAN

I'M UP SHORTLY AFTER 5:00 A.M., but it takes me 10 minutes just to start packing my bag. I'm sore. Stuffing my quilt, rolling my bivy, struggling with my shoes. Every movement is lethargic. I end up having to loosen my shoelaces because my feet are swelling. I can see my socks on both sides of my shoes' tongues now.

By the time I'm shuffling down the trail, it's already past 5:40. *I need to shorten this camp set-up/take-down process to only 15 minutes.* I've been able to do it in 20 minutes a few times since I started, but I know I can do it faster. *Shave 5 minutes off set-up and 5 minutes off take-down, and you've saved another half-mile.*

But it's amazing what sleep can do. I'm back to running. I'm beginning to come to terms with the pain in my feet. They hurt whether I walk or whether I run. *Guess I might as well run.* My watch goes off, letting me know I've hit my 30,000-step goal for the day.

Breakfast at a drive-through/walk-up coffee shop in Anacortes, past the marina, and the long way around an industrial complex. *At least it's all waterfront.* I can feel the sun being blocked out by a cloud. *Ah... shade. I love shade.* I look up to see this beautiful cloud I've envisioned and see a refinery directly below the sun, shooting smoke straight up to block it out. One would expect me to be upset with this pollutant.

But no. I'm grateful. *Thank you, smokestack.* I put my hands together and give a little bow. *Thank you for the shade.*

I message Sean Rutherford, aka Encore. He's been giving me live beta since he started the PNT earlier this summer. He's westbound. I'm eastbound. And we should be crossing each other's paths soon. He responds back. We're only a handful of miles from each other.

Soon I see him in the distance; we're already on the same side of the road. I raise my hands as I'm running toward him, silently wishing someone could film us running toward each other in slow motion through a field of wheatgrass with cinematic music in the background. It's good to see a familiar face.

We sit down in the shade of the only tree within sight. My legs are floating. This is the first time they've stopped since I was standing in the drive-through for my breakfast this morning. We munch on blackberries and share a couple of stories. Sean is gracious enough to ship a few of my unneeded items home for me—every time I go through a town, the post office is closed. I haven't been using my tarp stuff sack; I've just been rolling my tarp up and throwing it in my pack to save time. I haven't worn underwear since I swore it off due to the chafing 200 miles ago, and I don't need three pairs of socks; I have a fresh pair waiting for me at my next resupply. As I dig through my kit, handing Sean what I haven't used in several days, he asks if I have a rain kilt.

"No, just a rain jacket."

"You're going to want something for your legs on all the cold, wet bushwhacks coming up. Want to use mine?" He hands me his Zpacks DCF rain kilt.

"Are you sure?"

"If you'll use it, yeah, no problem. I don't think I'm going to need it anymore."

"Thank you!"

I look at my watch; it's already been 25 minutes. It seemed like only five. We say our goodbyes and get back to moving.

As I'm running across a bridge a few miles later, I see another backpacker headed in my direction from the other side. She definitely has that "thru-hiker" vibe, and why else would you be backpacking all these roads through the Puget Sound unless you were hiking the PNT?

"Are you hiking the PNT?"

"Yeah," she responds.

"Hell yeah!" I raise my hand and give her a high five as I pass her. She turns around and yells, "Are you *running* the PNT!?"

"Yeah!"

"F*** yeah you are!"

It's a fun 15-second interaction as we continue on our way. There's an excitement and energy that fellow thru-hikers on the same trail can share, even if they don't know each other and even if it's just for 15 seconds.

A few hours later, I'm charging my devices at The Cob and Cork in Edison, a fancy restaurant for such a small town. It's the only restaurant open right now; otherwise, I would be deterred by it. I feel out of place, underdressed. I know I stink. My white shirt is fading to brown. But the staff is fantastic. They don't seem to mind at all. I order the biggest breakfast meal on their menu. The owner makes me a free macchiato. One of the waitresses has always wanted to thru-hike; she keeps bringing me extra bread and tortillas from the back. As I'm packing up, I ask her, "Do you happen to know where I could find some sunscreen around here?"

She pauses, looks up, and then gives me the unfortunate news, "There's nothing out here. The only place that might have sunscreen is like eight miles out of your way." I thank her and get on my way.

A few buildings down is a shop with a big gas station sign out front. *Surely the gas station will have sunscreen.* As I get closer, I find out it's not a gas station. It's an old antiques and "stuff" store. I say "stuff" because it's nicer than saying "junk." The gas station sign is probably one of their items for sale. I walk in anyway and ask the owner, "Do you happen to have any sunscreen?"

He replies, "Does it look like we have any sunscreen here?"

As I'm about to respond, he interjects, "Wait… depends on how desperate you are."

"Do you see my arms?"

Normally I don't have to put sunscreen on. I spend so much time outside I haven't been burned while hiking in several years. But ever since I cut the sleeves off my shirt, my farmer's tan has been having quite the lifestyle change.

"I'll be right back." The old man walks toward the back of the store.

Another customer, wearing overalls, looks at me, then looks at my legs, then looks back up at me and says, "Your calves are like baseball bats."

"Thank you?"

The elderly man comes out from the back room with an old, dirty, half-used bottle of sunscreen with the label mostly missing. "Not sure if you want this. It's probably expired, but it's sunscreen. You can just have it."

"I'll take it! Thank you so much."

The upper backs of my arms are blistered. I've never seen so many bubbles from a sunburn before; it's the worst I've ever had. *At least it's in a small area.* I've been applying Aquaphor and Burt's Bees to the burns throughout the day, hoping they'd act as some kind of sunblock or skin protectant. I've also been tucking a corner of my microfiber towel under my backpack strap and letting the rest drape over my shoulder to block the sun on the worse of the two arms. But now I have *real* sunscreen. I coat it on thick as I'm walking down the road.

As soon as the sunblock is applied, I'm back to running. I start going up Oyster Dome, a rocky promontory in the Chuckanut Mountains, and I'm lifted with energy. I feel stronger. I'm powering through the ascents like it's day one. I've run the majority of my miles today, and I still feel fresh. Was it the 35-mile "rest" day yesterday? The loads of sleep last night? Maybe it's the big meal of real food I just ate that's giving me all this energy. Or maybe it's because I'm off paved roads and back in the mountains.

On the way up Oyster Dome, I meet another couple of thru-hikers. They call themselves the Himalayans. As their first thru-hike together, they completed the Great Himalaya Traverse, over 1,200 miles through some of the tallest mountains in the world. They're pretty down to earth and, as it turns out, extremely humble. I later find out that Kathleen Egan is an elite ultrarunner who takes first place in 200-mile races and has even made the front cover of running magazines. John Fiddler is a peak bagger who does wild fun stuff like kayaking hundreds of miles through the ocean. We chat for a couple of minutes. When they find out I've already done over 40 miles for the day, they ask, "Wait… are you trying to set an FKT?"

"I am, actually."

"Oh, you must be Encore's friend. He was telling us about you."

It turns out they had been hiking with my friend Sean over the previous few days. *Small world. The PNT is 1,248 miles long, but I guess it really is only a couple of feet wide.*

On my way back down the other side of Oyster Dome, I miss a turn. *There goes another hour. You've got to stop doing that, Nick.*

I'm back on more paved roads to connect the Oyster Dome foot trails with the Anderson Mountain trails. It's dusk now. I'll need to get my headlamp out soon. I try to hike as long as possible without using it to save battery. I usually make it a good 30 minutes past sunset before I need to turn it on. I pass another thru-hiker headed in the opposite direction. "PNT?" I point to him and ask.

"Yeah, you too?" he responds. "Where are you camping tonight?"

I jokingly, yet seriously, say, "The next flat spot I see."

He becomes silent, puts his head down, and marches on. He looks as tired as I am. He's probably just fishing for a possible camp spot, and my "next flat spot I see" comment isn't the answer he was looking for.

I'm out of water, and I'm already near 15 hours for the day. I've been telling myself I'd take it easy. And yet here I am, completely exhausted, continuing to hike forward. I check the map. The next designated camp spot is ten miles away, but I don't have the energy to travel three more hours tonight. I didn't realize the campsites on this trail are spread so far apart. *Great job, Nick. You've messed up again.* Squires Lake is just a few more miles ahead. *I'll filter water there. Maybe there'll be another flat spot on the trail next to it.*

As I reach the lake, I notice it's a day-use-only area. *What the hell? How is anyone supposed to hike this trail? There's nowhere to sleep.* I lean down to fill my water bottle next to a stream exiting the lake. It's been an hour since sunset, and I still haven't turned my headlamp on. The moon and stars are bright tonight. A frog jumps off a log into the water, nearly splashing me. I think I see a canoe on the far end of the small lake. Maybe someone is fishing? *I'm not supposed to be here. That means that canoe isn't supposed to be here either.* Maybe there isn't a canoe; maybe my eyes are just playing tricks on me. Luckily, the night sky is bright enough that I don't need my headlamp on, alerting others to my presence.

Less than 100 feet from where I get water is a wide-open grassy spot behind a tree. Its invitation is unquestionable. I'm too tired to move on, and it's calling my name. I spread out my bivy and bundle up inside my quilt. I'm thankful to be lying down. I'm thankful for another clear night. Lying down and staring up at the stars has become special to me.

BLACKBERRY BRAMBLES

I DON'T THINK that canoe ever existed. I never heard anyone getting out of the water last night, and there's no sign of a canoe as I'm walking around the lake. *My slow, quiet, non-headlamp motions last night were for nothing. I was trying to be stealthy for no reason at all.*

I'm tired, but I gain energy an hour into the climb up Anderson Mountain. I check my InReach tracker; it hasn't sent a single coordinate this morning yet. I've been moving for four hours, and my InReach claims I haven't moved a single foot. *Epic fail Garmin. Epic fail.* It just says, "Get a clear view of the sky," "Waiting for GPS signal," "Go outside to get a clear GPS signal." *I am outside you $300 paperweight.*

The trail out here on Anderson Mountain is *sometimes* marked with white blazes. It reminds me of the Appalachian Trail. Only the Appalachian Trail is one of the best-marked trails in the USA. The PNT is NOT.

I find more blackberries, but these are forbidden fruit. Tree farmers doused these woods with herbicides earlier this month. It's like someone holding candy in front of you and then saying, "Nope, can't have any."

Off the mountain and back on flats. *OK, I knew there were a lot of road walks out here, but I didn't think there would be this many.* A railroad parallels the road. I start walking the tracks to get off the hard, unforgiving pavement. It instantly feels like I'm on *The Walking Dead* headed toward a safe haven, only I'm by myself and no black-haired dreadlock lady with a samurai sword to save me. I am walking like a zombie now after all, so this seems fitting.

It's cold, windy, and misty on the way up and over Lyman Hill. I cinch the hood on my rain jacket a little tighter. The closer to the top of the mountain I get, the better I can see the islands of the Puget Sound off in the distance. They look so far away. *Wow. I was on the other side of that bay yesterday.*

I make it to the top. The trail becomes overgrown with vegetation again. It's only raining a light mist, but the bushes crowding out the trail are soaked. I zip up the rain kilt that Sean loaned me as well as my waterproof calf gaiters. *I'm staying dry today!* At least that's what I tell myself. My shoes are already getting wet from all the water coming off the plants and running down my legs.

As I continue along a decommissioned forest service road that's slowly being swallowed up by the forest, I eventually lose the path. Apparently other people have before too. I've followed a social trail in the wrong direction until the path completely disappeared. I check the map. *Yup, I'm off track—again.* I head back where I came from, holding my phone up with the GPS on so I can find where the trail turned off of the abandoned, barely noticeable road. I make it to where the GPS suggests I need to turn, but I don't see the trail. *I guess I go that way?*

I work my way through wet bushes taller than I am. *Thank you for loaning me your rain kilt, Sean. Thank you.* After a half-mile of slow off-trail travel—sometimes feeling like I'm walking where other humans have walked before and other times questioning myself—I decide there has to be a more distinct path somewhere. I keep checking the map, it indicates I'm precisely on the trail. *This can't be right. This isn't even labeled as a bushwhack section.*

I've been following a small ridgeline of trees. I climb up the ridge for a better view, hoping to be able to see a well-carved trail somewhere. As soon as I make it to the top there's an obvious trail directly on the other side not even 50 feet away. I shake my head. *I've been walking through all this junk, while the trail is literally right beside me.* Most hikers are headed westbound, and because of that—despite the PNT not being very well marked to begin with—it's easier to follow for westbounders, better indicators. I'm headed east, and I'm certainly feeling the difference.

After less than a mile of travel on this newly found trail, the rain slows and the clouds drop into a thick fog. I can't see farther than 20 feet ahead. The bushes have dissipated, and I'm surrounded by tall, slender trees. It feels like a fairytale. I see the back end of a black bear running away. It must have seen me first. *Seriously, their butts are so fluffy!* It quickly escapes into the dense fog before I can get my phone out for a picture.

As I'm nearing the other side of the mountain another trailless section comes up. It's only one mile long, but it's straight through blackberries the entire way. *A bushwhack through blackberry brambles? Who the hell picked this route?* I begin to think it's on purpose. *Of course they'd throw in a bushwhack littered with thorns.* A normal bushwhack isn't good enough for the PNT. Let's go through shards of glass.

As I'm weaving my way through, I realize it could be worse. I'm making better time than I thought I would. It's still slow movement, don't get me wrong, but there's been enough foot traffic through here this year that there's actually a little bit of a trail forming. A makeshift path has been cleared—I just have to stay sleek and agile enough to avoid the thorns. Plus there's an added bonus: If at any moment you get too sick and tired of the briars tearing away at your skin, just take a break and eat all the berries your heart desires.

Once I reach the base of the mountain the sun has already gone down, and I'm beyond tired. The tendon between the top of my left foot and shin is tight and tender. *I need to spend extra time rolling that out.* As I move one foot in front of the other, I try to decide where I'll stop for camp. I'd like to at least make it part of the way up Mount Josephine. *The farther I go today, the tomorrow-me will thank myself.*

After a few switchbacks up an old forest service road that's slowly evolved into a hiking trail, I come across a flat spot. *I'll take it.* I sweep a few twigs and debris away to clear a spot for my bivy. It's not raining anymore, but I can't see the stars and it still *feels* like rain. *I'll bet those are still rain clouds. I'm setting up the tarp tonight.*

The ground is hard. I pick up a rock to help hammer my tent stakes into the ground. As I'm nailing the last stake into the ground, the head of it breaks off. *This ground must be the shoulder of the old forest service road. It's probably all hard compact gravel.* At least it's only the head of the stake; the rest of it is still usable.

I spend an hour between massaging my feet and trying to work out the stiffness in my left shin. As I turn over after stretching my ankle, I slip off my bivy and my hand squishes a slug. If you've ever hiked in the Pacific Northwest you know what kind of slug I'm talking about. These things are monsters, oftentimes longer and fatter than your middle finger. And that's exactly what this giant booger's doing—giving me the middle finger. My hand is slimy and sticky. The slug is gone, but its remnants remain. I wipe my hand on the grass and scout the perimeter for any more of his brothers and sisters. *The coast is clear. Time to get some sleep.*

MUD

WHEN I OPEN MY EYES the next morning, I hear rain sprinkling on my tarp. I check the time. My alarm hasn't even gone off yet. I can afford another hour of rest. I close my eyes and try to go back to sleep, but my mind is preoccupied. I can't stop thinking about the rain, my wet shoes, my broken tent stake, and the day I have ahead. I text Hannah, asking her to add a tent stake to the next resupply box before I forget and lose cell service again.

By 6:00 a.m., the rain has stopped. I try to pack up quickly, but my two pure carbon fiber tent stakes are stuck in the ground. The four aluminum carbon core stakes come out much more easily, even the one with the broken head from last night. After spending a good five minutes trying to get one out, I end up breaking it in half. Soon I snap the other carbon fiber tent stake. *Great, how am I supposed to pitch my tarp with half my stakes broken? I should have brought the mini-groundhogs.* I'm beating myself up for choosing lighter weight over greater durability on the tent stakes.

I text Hannah, "Never mind. Add six of the mini-groundhogs to the next box. I just broke two more stakes." I check the map. My Ross Lake resupply box is already there; the next box Hannah is sending will be in Oroville, 300 miles away. *Six-ish more days till I can get more tent stakes.*

By 8:00 a.m., a misty drizzle has returned, and the fog is so thick I can barely see 20 feet in front of me. I hear chainsaws buzzing in the distance—Mount Josephine tree farmers. It's surprisingly peaceful. The fog is calming.

But the calm always comes before the storm.

Going down Mount Josephine on the other side absolutely sucks. The rain grows heavier. The trail, the overgrown plants, my glasses, my bag—everything is covered in a blanket of wet.

As I'm charging through a nasty bushwhack with seemingly endless blowdowns, I have to take the rain kilt off to be able to lift my legs high enough to maneuver over and around the fallen giants. My GPS and phone screen are soon inoperable in the rain.

Next, the trail disappears. I somehow get my GPS to work again for a few seconds, despite the constant rain on the screen. I'm way off track, frustrated and exhausted. *I must have followed a game trail in the wrong direction.* As I work my way back toward where I should be headed, my right foot sinks up to my knee in a deep bog. It's a mud pit covered by green moss, disguised as solid ground. Inertia pushes me forward; now my left foot is caught in a vacuum. I quickly lift my right foot, momentum still carrying me forward. I'm trying not to faceplant. My right shoe stays behind as my leg comes out. My gaiter, attached to my ankle and shoe, rips apart as my foot escapes. My foot, now shoeless, goes back into the mire. I've caught my balance, but I'm stuck.

I look around. *How did I end up in a muddy marsh?* I feel like I'm already halfway through the worst of it; there's higher ground just a few steps away. *If I can just make it a couple more steps.* The suction from the muck holds onto my feet. It's hard to lift either foot. When I lift one leg to bring it out, the other is driven in deeper. *How am I going to get out of this?*

I reach into the hole for my lost shoe. Luckily, it isn't hard to find. I pull it out and sling gunk out of it. The side of my shirt and arm are now covered in sludge. I kneel down and use my entire right shin to distribute weight more evenly across the pit, like a snowshoe, instead of just my bare, muddy-socked foot. I try to lift my left foot straight out instead of bending at the ankle, so I don't lose my other shoe and tear my other gaiter. I'm still sinking in, but not as deep. I'm slowly able to crawl my way out and make it to solid ground.

I'm covered in mud. *I must look like Arnold Schwarzenegger hiding from the Predator, minus the muscles.*

I scrape the filth off myself and shake my hands to fling it away. I put my right shoe back on, leaving my half-torn gaiter flopping off to the side, and slog forward. Luckily, the rain is helping wash everything off.

My spirit is broken. I feel like I'm lost. My GPS isn't working. Paper maps are worthless in the rain. Everything is wet, and I'm covered in slop. I'm exhausted, physically and emotionally. I struggle to climb over blowdowns scattered through more muddy marshes. It's impossible to move fast. I scream into the woods as loud as I can. Tears run down my face.

Just keep moving. And so I keep moving. But I don't do it quietly.

"F*** you trees."

"F*** you mountain."

"F*** you trail."

"No… F*** you *nonexistent* trail."

I'm thankful I'm in the middle of the woods with no one around to see or hear me. I'm a little kid throwing a temper tantrum. *Some self-control I have.* Embarrassed and ashamed, I trudge forward. *Don't cuss at the woods, Nick. It's disrespectful to the mountains.*

I come up over a hill and see the light appearance of a trail forming down below. *I'm back on track.* Once I reach the trail, I follow it for about 100 feet before it's gone again.

The downed trees are so big I can't see over them even whilst laying on their sides. With the whopping mess of branches, vines, moss, and other debris scattered across the trees, they seem wider than I am tall. It takes several minutes just to get over one. *This is taking forever.*

Over, under, around. Down through the hole in the ground the roots left when the tree was uprooted, and back up the other side. The trees have left root holes so massive it takes over 10 steps to get across them. Every time I make it across a downed tree, I'm left searching for the trail on the other side.

All of a sudden, I see a pink ribbon tied to a tree limb. I don't think anything of it at first, but as I keep navigating the obstacle course of a trail I see another pink ribbon over a hundred feet away. And then another, and another. It dawns on me. *The trail is marked out here!* A prayer is answered, and all of a sudden the path is easier to follow. I feel confident I'm headed in the right direction, even though I can't confirm with my map in the cold rain.

Aside from the blowdowns, the ground is quite soft. It's spongey. My feet seem to be feeling better. They don't ache quite as bad, and the massaging I did to my shin last night must be working because there's less pain there as well.

As soon as the trail clears up, I'm back to running. I'm even running some of the uphills. It's such a relief to be able to move quickly again. I no longer have to fight the jungle. I no longer have to navigate. All I have to do is move.

By the time I near the top of the trail on Mount Baker, I find a shelter. I step inside to wring out my socks and give my feet some air time. I find a few short pieces of metal that could work as makeshift tent stakes until I can actually replace my broken ones. At least I hope they will work as tent stakes. They're more like large staples. They aren't very long. They might not work. But they're better than nothing.

The rain slows, and the clouds drop. I welcome it. I'm normally a big fan of fog, but I'm ecstatic about it now. The shroud of mist means it's not raining hard anymore.

I make my way up and over the highest point of the day, switchbacks up a boulder and talus slope. I can't see any trees. There is zero visibility in this cloud. I should be able to see the crown of Mount Baker from here. It should be right in my face, but all I see is a wall of white. *What a beautiful view of Mount Baker on this super clear and sunny day.*

According to the comments on Guthooks, there's a campground at the bottom of the mountain with a bathroom that has electricity. It's six more miles than what my goal was for the day, but it has a DRY bathroom. It's only a matter of time before it starts raining again, and I don't even know if these small, nail-sized pieces of metal I found will be strong enough to hold my tarp up. *I could sleep dry tonight AND charge everything while I sleep.*

Motivation of a dry bathroom quickens my pace. Full throttle, I'm on the fast track to get there in no time.

Trip, CRASH!!

I trip over the smallest root, barely even protruding from the trail, and faceplant on the ground.

I lie there and moan. The palms of my hands are roughed up, but not quite bleeding. I inspect my rain jacket, half expecting the elbows to be shredded. Everything is intact. *Thank you.* I stand up, brush myself off, adjust my crooked glasses, and start moving—at a much slower pace.

By the time I make it to the campground, it's past 11:00 p.m. The rain has stopped, and the fog is patchy. I run into the bathroom. *There's a hand blow dryer in here!* I plug in my electronics and start to dry off my shorts, socks, and towel. *I'm going to have dry socks tomorrow!* I'm so exhausted I sleep right next to the bathroom. I don't even bother setting up my tarp. *If it starts raining I'll just go sleep inside.* Before I know it, I'm out cold.

DIZZY

BITTER, DAMP EARLY MORNING temperatures wake me up. It's just after 3:00 a.m. I'm not in a legal campsite next to this bathroom. This is a paid campground area. I need to get out of here before anything becomes a problem. Last night, I kept imagining someone walking to the bathroom and then trying to shoo off this homeless-looking person sleeping beside it.

My feet have still been aching throughout the night, making it hard to sleep, but I feel like I'm slowly getting used to it. The pain is becoming more dull.

As I'm packing up and sliding on my shoes and socks, I realize I didn't live up to the task of drying everything out last night. I must have been too tired to realize how poor of a job I was doing. My shoes and socks are still wet.

The mileage around Baker Lake is a good morning surprise. The gentle, rolling trail meticulously finds its way along the steep mountain forming the eastern bank of the lake. The trails are clean, mostly flat, and maintained. *What a blessing after yesterday's mess.* The cooler temperatures and fog are making me fast. I'm making excellent time, but I still can't see Mount Baker. I can barely even see Baker Lake; the fog is so thick.

I must have lost my Burt's Bees in the storm yesterday. It's not in my pocket anymore.

By 9:45 a.m., the sun is out in full force for the first time in days. It's a little early in the day for a break, but I decide to take this opportunity to dry out my gear. I find a large downed tree, half of which is being used as a bridge for a stream crossing. The tree becomes my drying rack. I lay everything out: socks, shoes, insoles, tarp, rain gear, gaiters. Even the bottom of my bivy needs to dry.

With the full power of the sun and good gear, everything is dry within 10 minutes—except my shoes. They're still damp, but much better than they were. I pack up and get moving.

A few miles later, there's another heavy stream crossing with a tree across it to function as a bridge. Only this tree bridge isn't nearly the size of the other one. The narrow end of it is only five inches in diameter. If it weren't for the fact that a trail crew had shaved the top side of the tree down to make it flat for walking on, I would have never thought it was a footbridge—it just looks like a small tree that fell over in the last storm. *We're supposed to walk across that? I freaking love this trail.* And no, I'm not being sarcastic. It's not just hiking; it's a full-on adventure! *Ha! I say I love it, but yesterday I was cussing it out.*

Onward and upward I go as I keep climbing toward the Mount Baker ski area. The fog is gone; the clouds have lifted. I can finally see the bottom half of the crown of Mount Baker. It's bigger than I imagined. The top of it is still hidden by clouds, but the glaciers surrounding the peak are monolithic.

A few miles later, I hear rustling up ahead. I look up the trail and see a cloven, white-bearded wizard charging off into the brush, horns first. *Less than 24 hours on Mount Baker and I've already seen a mountain goat!*

The vegetation surrounding the trail is back to overgrown and wet. The leaves saturate my legs. The water runs down into my trail runners. My socks soak it up like a sponge until they can't hold anymore and are left swimming in the pools of water inside my shoes.

As I'm climbing the 4,000-foot ascent toward the Mount Baker Ski Area, I feel completely drained two miles from the top. My pace plummets. I'm looking forward to that downhill flow on the other side of the mountain.

My lips begin to feel tingly. I'm dizzy. Lightheaded. *No, not here. Not now.* I've had issues with electrolytes, dehydration, and heat in the past. Earlier this year, when I attempted to break the Ouachita Trail FKT, I failed miserably. One of those attempts ended after I couldn't hold down fluids—and that night of misery started with tingly lips.

Opening my mouth is a slow process. My whole face is tingling now. I open and shut my mouth, somehow thinking that exercising those muscles will work it out, and I'll have full function of my lips again. I look like a fish. *I'll stop and take a break at this parking lot up here.*

When I make it to the parking lot—there are trash cans! To say I have a newfound appreciation for a place to put waste is an understatement. I dump my trash, lightening my load and clearing my pockets.

I sit down on a bench and kick off my shoes. A snack and two salt pills later, I'm inspecting my feet. They've been wet for so long they're no longer just wrinkly; they have tiny dark pits forming in them. I try to wipe my feet clean with my towel, but the black spots inside these little pits won't wipe off. It almost looks like mold is growing on the bottom of my feet.

I lie down as I look up at the sky. *I'll just rest here for 20 minutes until I'm feeling better.*

Forty minutes pass before I'm back on my feet.

That break did me good. I feel like I'm crushing the mileage. *This is the fastest I've moved since I started the PNT!* Usually I'm averaging between three and four miles per hour, but I tackle the next 10 in less than two.

Ha. I softly laugh. *Funny how I can go from dizzy and woozy to having an absolute blast running for 10 miles straight.*

The path finishes its descent and flattens out, but not for long. Soon I'm on my way uphill toward Hannegan Pass.

I check the map. It's time to decide where I'm going to stop for the night. At the Hannegan Pass trailhead shelter? Or do I make it all the way across the pass to a low-elevation campsite since it's supposed to be cold tonight? If I choose the latter, it'll end up being a 56-mile day. *Not sure I'm ready for that.* I make my decision. I'm going for the shorter of the two options, the shelter. It'll block more wind and allow for better rest during the frigid night that's supposed to be coming. It's already cold, and the sun isn't even down yet. I love it.

I thrive in cooler temperatures. Heat is my kryptonite. If it's 100 degrees out, it seems like I can't make it five miles. But throw me on a snow-capped mountain, and I feel like I can go forever.

The forest on the way up the mountain is quiet yet teeming with life. The way the light breaks through the canopy is sublime. The greens are abundant and rich. The air is invigorating. It's an ambiance that can only be experienced in person to be truly understood. Describing it is a disservice.

I come across a massive tree stump—what's left of a behemoth of a tree that clearly died a long time ago. A couple of full-sized trees are growing out of it. *The dead doesn't die out here.*

I make it to the shelter as the sun is setting. It has a cold concrete floor. My face changes from a dull, tired smile to a disappointed frown. As I walk under the roof, I notice a sudden, faint movement in a dark corner. *Great.* The last time I slept in a high-traffic campsite, I ended up swearing off heavily used areas because mice were annoying me all night. But I've already committed to this spot, and I know it'll be warmer with the wind protection from the shelter than without it.

There's a wooden picnic table partially under the shelter. *If I sleep on top of that, it would keep me off the cold concrete floor and farther away from the mice.* I drag the table into the shelter a few more feet. It's heavy; it's built to last. I pull it in just enough to have protection from the wind on three sides.

On top of the picnic table, I slip my quilt inside my bivy. The bivy always adds another five degrees of warmth. I put on all my layers—long sleeve shirt, rain jacket, puffy jacket. I'm going to stay warm tonight.

Thinking about the day and thinking about tomorrow, it's refreshing to know I've put in 49 miles before the sun even set. I'll have plenty of time to rest and recover tonight. Tomorrow should be strong.

---- DAY 11 ----

MUSHROOMS

I OPEN MY EYES. I see mouse poop.

I'm lying down on my side on top of the picnic table I drug under the shelter last night. Mouse turds are forming a perimeter around me. I didn't hear them once last night. I was tired. I slept hard all night long. Best sleep I've had since I started the PNT.

As I pack my bag, I inspect for evidence of mice tampering with my gear. I hung everything up last night to be proactive, and I'm thankful I did. I don't see any damage.

I'm up and over Hannegan Pass and into North Cascades National Park fairly quickly. North Cascades is one of my favorite national parks, but I've never been on this side of it. The forest here is thicker, more lush. Moss, trees, ferns, and mushrooms—so many mushrooms. It's a mystical place. Reminds me of *FernGully*. I'm losing time because I'm stopping to take so many pictures. *But I want a picture of every single species of mushroom out here.*

As I'm approaching the Chilliwack River, I see a two-story wooden structure. It has cables hanging from it, stretching across to an equal wooden structure on the other side. It's a cable car crossing! My eyes light up. I get all giddy like a kid in a candy store. I've never seen one of these in real life, and now I get to cross a stream in it!

I climb up the ladder to the top of the stand. The cable car is a two-person metal basket. Hikers can sit on either side of each other, with just enough room for their legs and packs in the middle. I pull the car back toward the tower just a bit, step in, and off I go. It's easier to move than I thought it would be. All it takes is one hand pulling back on the rope, and the car just glides along. The giant pulleys on either end make easy work of crossing the stream. If it weren't for the fact that I'm out here trying to set a speed record, I would probably ride the cable car back and forth several times. It's like a manually operated amusement ride!

When I near the top of Whatcom Pass, my eyes widen. Views of the Cascades extend for miles in all directions. Waterfalls crash down the sides of the mountains seemingly everywhere, connecting with the rivers in the deep valley below. And then there are the glaciers. I'm a sucker for a good glacier. There's something just so liberating about massive chunks of ice. They free you from the shackles of society.

The Challenger Glacier is hanging on the edge of the mountain in a slow-motion slide off a cliff that will take unknown lifetimes to complete. I can only imagine how tall the sheer wall of ice is at the base of it. It's distant but still looks absolutely monstrous compared to some of the other glaciers I've explored. I imagine what a person would look like if they were on it, an itty bitty ant-sized figure climbing up the wall.

I keep ascending the trail. It gets narrower and narrower; eventually it disappears. *I should have been over the pass by now.* I check my map. *Oh… that's why. I'm not on the trail anymore.* I've missed my turn and followed a spur trail up toward an overlook. Great spot for a break and a chance to dry off some sweaty, wet clothes, though.

On the way down Whatcom Pass, I'm introduced to "Whatcom's Wiggles." I'm not sure if the switchbacks down the mountain actually have a name or not, but they are epic enough to be named—so I've given them a name. If you've ever hiked Angel's Landing in Zion National Park, think about the switchbacks on Walter's Wiggles. Then think even more. Longer. And steeper. Forty-three switchbacks, to be exact, carved into the side of a steep mountain face. With all the lumber used to retain the walls of the cliffside trail, it reminds me of a ladder. *Thank goodness I'm headed east.* I'm thankful I'm not having to climb up this. The ascent on the other side of the mountain didn't seem this dramatic.

Just as I'm getting spoiled with clean, well-maintained trails in North Cascades National Park, I hit an extremely overgrown section. I swim my way through the thick bushes and leaves; it lasts for miles. *This trail is teaching me to have a newfound respect for trail maintenance. At least it's fairly quick moving.* The trail below the leaves and out of sight is free of roots or rocks that would otherwise be hidden tripping hazards. And the leaves are dry! This is some of the most overgrown trail I've encountered, but it's surprisingly pleasant to move through—it's not dripping wet.

Hours later, I run into a maintenance crew clearing the trails. Six feet out on either side are perfectly trimmed to the ground. They tell me I should have clean walking for the next 10 miles. *Sweet.*

Down the mountain, across the valley, and up toward Beaver Pass, I hear someone sneeze off in the distance. I assume they're at the Beaver Pass camp since I haven't seen anyone on trail in a while. I yell, "Bless you!" And a couple of seconds later, I hear a faint yell back, "Thank you!"

Three passes today: Hannegan, Whatcom, and Beaver. My body is ready to be done. I check the map. Only a few more hours to go tonight. My next resupply is at Ross Lake Resort, and there's no way I'll make it before they close, so my plan is to camp a handful of miles away and then get there right when they open in the morning.

Next, I see the national park boundary post. *Made it through North Cascades National Park in 10 hours! Ross Lake, here I come.*

Frogs are everywhere. Big frogs. Lots of really, really big frogs. *They're called toads, Nick.* I almost step on one. *These monsters are as big as my feet!* Maybe they come out at dusk, or maybe there's a plague going on, but the mushrooms of the North Cascades have definitely been replaced by the frogs of Ross Lake.

When the sun goes down, so does my energy. I keep tripping over rocks and roots. My eyes keep closing. The blinks get longer and longer, till I can no longer use the excuse that I'm blinking—so I open them as wide as possible in an attempt to force them to stay awake. I'm so tired I have to slap myself in the face just to keep from falling asleep. I keep looking at my watch. *It's only been two minutes? How has it only been two minutes?!* The next hour seems like five.

The next designated campsite is off the main trail, near the shore of Ross Lake. I've made the turn, but it seems like the spur trail to access it just keeps going on forever. Any amount of distance away from the PNT always seems outrageously long, even if it's just three-tenths of a mile. My feet are toast. My body is spent. I can't believe I'm having to go so far out of the way. I come across the fire ring and cooking area. The tent sites are still farther down the hill, but I see a flat spot. *Who cares if this isn't a designated camp spot. I'll be gone before sun-up. No one will ever know I was here.*

WOULD COME BACK HERE AGAIN

I DIDN'T SLEEP WELL last night next to the fire ring. A mouse has discovered this food prep area is a reliable source of scraps—and it thought I had snacks. *Saving the extra five minutes of not going to the designated tent site and sleeping next to the fire ring wasn't worth it. I should have known that.* But last night, I just didn't want to go any farther. I was struggling to stay awake. I stopped because it was a flat and open enough spot to lie down in.

I sleep in as long as possible—the sun is my signal. Only five more miles to Ross Lake Resort, but there's no need to get there before they open. *I hope the resort has some tent stakes and a microfiber towel.* Some cheap tent stakes would work better than these short pieces of scrap metal I found in the shelter on Mount Baker. But what's possibly worse, I lost my towel yesterday—again. My back-chafe-saving microfiber towel. The resort has a small store, minimal options, but I'm crossing my fingers.

The next few miles of trail are filled with bridge crossings over canyon-carved streams and vistas of Ross Lake that just tease you. The forest is so thick the trees block a majority of the view. I can see just enough of the lake to know I want to see more.

I roll into Ross Lake Resort just before they open their doors. The entire resort consists of 15 floating cabins and a small marina, only accessible by hiking in or riding a boat across the lake. It's a fascinating place that can cost a small fortune for most visitors, but I get to experience it for free. Two people are already waiting in line for them to open, so I'm third. Once the main office opens, I look around the store for towels or tent stakes—I see neither. But I see candy. That's how the stores get you. They always put the candy right where you're standing in line to check out. *These Starbursts and Skittles are coming with me.*

Once I'm at the counter, I ask for my resupply box and confirm they don't have any towels or stakes. The lady helping me explains they do have a hiker box, though. A hiker box is a beautiful system. It saves people the weight of not having to carry something they no longer require, while potentially saving another hiker in desperate need. Sick of carrying something? Don't want it anymore? But it still holds enough value that it shouldn't be thrown away? Stick it in a hiker box. Maybe tomorrow's hiker will need it.

I sit down at a picnic table near an outlet to charge my tech while I go through my resupply and dig through the tub of "give a penny, take a penny" hiker supplies. As I open the bin, the very first item I see, sitting right on top smiling at me, is a microfiber towel! *Ah! Yes! Manna from heaven again!* I shovel down an entire can of Salt and Vinegar Pringles, two muffins, five cupcakes, two root beers, and a Gatorade before getting back on the trail.

My brand-new shoes from my resupply box are super cushy on my feet. I'm walking on clouds. Dry, fresh, clean socks. New gaiters to replace the ones I'd broken. I'm grateful. The bottom of my feet are still pruney from the multiple days of rain around Mount Josephine and Mount Baker. The little circular pits that look like mold is growing in them don't appear to be getting any better, but I have dry shoes now.

I instantly feel the weight of my pack pushing me toward the earth. Gravity is working overtime. This is the second longest food carry I'll have of the entire trip: through the Ross Lakes area, the Pasayten Wilderness, and the miles and miles of roads to get into Oroville, WA. Despite everything I just ate before leaving the resort, I try to eat as much food as possible, as soon as possible, to lighten my load while moving. I stuff food into my mouth, nonstop, until my stomach just can't take any more. I'm looking forward to a couple of days going by, so my pack will be lighter.

Miles later, I lean down next to a stream to refill a water bottle.

Slip and *SPLASH!*

As I'm filling my bottle, one of my feet slips off a rock and into the stream. Unnecessary wet shoe. *At least it's only one foot.*

The trail along the northeastern shore of Ross Lake rewards me with the views I've been wanting. A cliff on one side, a narrow footpath, and a short drop-off into the water on the other. It's the first time I've been able to see a substantial portion of the reservoir unobscured, aside from the resort and dam area.

As I leave the Ross Lake National Recreation Area and enter the Pasayten Wilderness, I'm instantly met with blown-down trees across the trail. One tree has even taken out the Pasayten Wilderness sign. I imagine a Ross Lake trail crew employee getting to the end of their responsibilities, looking at the sign, and thinking, "Nope. My job finishes here. I don't have to touch anything on that side." *I should come back out here with tools another time to do some trail maintenance myself.*

I first hear, and then spot a black bear munching on berries right beside the trail. It glances up, then scurries up the hill to get away. It doesn't go far before turning around to huff and puff at me. I can't see it in the thick brush anymore; I can only hear it chuffing. *This definitely looks like bear country.* The hillsides are steep for a human, a piece of cake for a bear. Thick bushes full of berries cover the mountainside, with trees scattered about.

I keep hiking up Devil's Dome. It's a strenuous 5,000-foot climb. I'm back in the wilderness and haven't seen anyone in hours. It's midafternoon. The sun is cooking. The sweat begins to drip. *Not today, chafing.* The shorts come off to keep them dry.

As I near the top of the mountain, the views of Ross Lake and the Western Cascades begin to open. Greens and blues and shadowy hues. Clouds take shape, spilling across the sky. And then, bam! I run into a hiker. *I'm caught in the nude again.* He's sitting down in the middle of the trail, taking a break, while looking out over Ross Lake. As soon as I see him, I jump backward and step off into the bushes to put my shorts back on.

When I get back on trail and walk toward him, he shouts, "Oh! I thought you were a bear at first."

"No, but I did see a bear down the trail not too long ago. I thought you had just caught me hiking in the nude; that's why I went off into the bushes." I laugh. (You see, if you call yourself out on the embarrassing moments, they're a little easier to bear. No pun intended.) I explain why I didn't have my shorts on—I'm not just some nudist frolicking around in the forest.

"Oh no, I never saw you, ha! I was looking at the lake when I thought I heard a bear in the bushes. Then you came around the corner."

Facepalm. "You mean to tell me I didn't even have to call myself out for hiking naked?"

"No," he laughs. He goes on to tell me how he's heard that Vagisil is the best form of chafing protection for men.

"Interesting…" *What if I started asking random strangers for Vagisil? "Hey, can I borrow some Vagisil? Just a little bit? I just need a little bit of Vagisil."*

As it turns out, he's a PCT hiker who had come off the trail earlier in the year, and he's headed back to finish it. His trail name is Happy Hour. When he was going through the deserts of Southern California on the PCT, people kept giving him cold beers. It happened so often, Happy Hour was born.

We say our goodbyes and good wishes, and I continue on up the mountain.

The views of Jack Mountain approaching the top of Devil's Dome damn near make me pee my pants—it's ok though, because I'm not wearing any. The higher I climb, the more detailed the mountain becomes—predominantly towering over the valley. Rusty reds and yellows on the ground clash with the vibrant evergreens. White glaciers pop with contrast as more and more shadows appear. *Would come back here again.* I wish I could stop here for the night to watch the sunset. I keep pausing to take pictures—it's killing my time.

Suddenly, my path ends. I've reached the summit. I check the map. I'm off-trail… again. The PNT took a turn not too far back; it didn't actually go all the way to the top of Devil's Dome. But the views… *Worth it.*

As I head down the other side of the mountain, the sun reaches its golden hour. The sky is covered by a blanket of dark clouds, but just at the edge of the horizon, the clouds open up to let the glow of a light orange sunset peek through. The jagged peaks of the Cascade Mountains extend as far as I can see in all directions. Up close, the silhouettes of evergreens give perspective to the size of the mountains and forests in the distance. I begin to hear thunder crackling from the west, where I just came from. The clouds thicken and darken even more. *It's going to rain soon.*

Thoughts about tomorrow and the rest of the trail start to fill my mind. I'm only a few days away from the halfway point—728 miles left. I do the math in my head. I could finish in 28 days, but I can't mess it up with any more low-mileage days. Time to start getting up at 4:00 a.m. from now on.

I turn a corner to see a captivating tent site. It's sheltered by a crescent of trees on one side and has an open view of the Cascade Mountains for miles on the other. Two guys are sitting on logs around a campfire. They look at me with guilty faces. One of them seems to be holding his breath. And then *Poof.* Out of his mouth comes a cloud of smoke. Then I notice the pipe he's holding in his hand. *Busted!*

Onward down the mountain I go. I still have 10 more miles before my goal campsite, but heaps of dead trees are scattered across the trail, and it's getting dark. At least they're fairly easy to navigate around. It just takes more time.

Dear God, there are a lot of blowdowns. *OK, they aren't easy to get around anymore.*

A light rain begins. It slowly but steadily becomes heavier and heavier. It's dark. *Why are there so many blowdowns?!* They just don't stop. They're relentless. They don't get tired—I do. I keep stepping off the trail, tripping and falling. My pace is weakening.

I make it over another pass and down into a basin. I come across a flat spot in the trail. I check the map. I'm at mile 527. I originally wanted to make it to the trail camp three miles farther, but I'm moving so slow I feel like it'll be well past 11:30 p.m. before I make it there, possibly midnight. *I'll stop here.*

I pitch my tarp in the middle of the trail and dive under to escape the rain. Hunched over, in my four-foot-wide, four-foot-tall living space that pyramids to a point at the top, not allowing much room for my shoulders when sitting, I unroll my sleep setup and scoot it underneath myself. As I begin massaging my feet before sleep, my headlamp battery dies. *Perfect timing.*

THE LAND OF 1,000 BLOWDOWNS

LAST NIGHT WAS COLD. I've been sleeping with my electronics in my quilt so the temperatures won't drain the batteries prematurely. I wake up just a few minutes before my alarm goes off at 4:00 a.m. *Guess it's time to get moving.*

I start packing up camp while thinking about the day ahead. I took lots of pictures yesterday; I need to take fewer to make sure I have enough battery to get out of the Pasayten Wilderness. With how much traveling I'm doing in the dark, having power for my headlamp is critical. I need my InReach for FKT verification. And with how rarely trail junctions are marked for the PNT, I need my phone for GPS. GPS is substantially faster than navigating by paper map.

Soon I'm on the Pacific Crest Trail. The PNT travels along the PCT for roughly 14 miles, from Holman Pass to Castle Pass. *Ah, this PCT section is so clean and maintained. This is nice.* First time to get some solid running in since entering the Pasayten.

There's significantly more traffic on the PCT. I'm passing hikers nearly every mile. I pass a couple of hikers on a downhill section. One of them raises their hand to give me a high five and yells, "Hell yeah, brother! Nice run!" The encouragement makes me move faster. *This trail has energy.*

I come up behind another hiker on the way up a pass. She turns around, "Congratulations on your hike!" Most people on the PCT headed north here are about to finish their 2,650-mile journey. The end of the PCT, Canada, is just a few hours ahead. She thinks I'm hiking the PCT.

"Thank you, but I'm actually just getting started. I still have another 700 miles to go. I'm hiking the PNT, not the PCT."

"I'm hiking the PNT too! No one else out here knows what the PNT is; I have to keep explaining it." She continues, "I've already done the majority of the trail, but I skipped the Pasayten this summer, so I've come back to finish it."

"Nice! Congratulations on YOUR hike!" I respond. It's even more energizing to meet another PNT hiker.

I find out her trail name is Poppy. I still don't have one. Mark, a fellow hiking enthusiast who just so happens to be married to my mom, called me "Buff" since I was caught hiking "in the buff," but that sounds too much like a bodybuilder. I don't want to be known as Arnold Schwarzenegger prancing around in the forest. Then he wanted to call me "Flash," because I flashed people. But I also don't want to be associated with a superhero running around in tight red spandex. Besides that, Mark isn't on the trail. He's at home in Missouri. I feel like your trail name should come "from" the trail.

The trail skirts the ridgeline of the mountains from pass to pass, revealing its finest. Running is smooth and easy. It's well graded. It's engaging. It's fun. Enough trees are scattered for character, but you're up high enough that you can see for miles. The trail charges me, lights me up with energy. I wonder what it would be like thru-hiking the PCT. *Is the PCT this pretty and this clean the whole way?*

The PCT is the trail I've been dreaming of. I have maps of it on the walls in our house. I've read books about it. I've even scouted well over 200 miles of it. Everything I've seen has been jaw-droppingly beautiful. *This is where I was supposed to be.* I imagine arriving at the northern terminus of the PCT, at the border of Canada, just four miles north of Castle Pass. *No. Everything happens for a reason. You're supposed to be on the PNT. You're doing exactly what you're supposed to be doing.*

As soon as I'm off the PCT, I'm back to masses of windthrow. If I'm not climbing over blowdowns, crawling under them, or navigating around them—I guess this isn't the Pasayten Wilderness. *They should call this the land of 1,000 blowdowns.* Every time I crawl under a dead tree on all fours I just want to lie down on the ground and stay there.

As I'm climbing over what must be the hundredth dead tree that hour, I trip and tumble over it. *OK, new rule. Stop slipping on blowdowns and stabbing yourself in the leg.*

My legs are bleeding. My body is sore. I'm tired. I've fallen more times than I care to remember. At least it's really overcast. *God is blocking the sun from beating down on me since there are enough blowdowns beating up on me.*

I faceplant when trying to climb over another collapsed tree. *OK, you have slipped and fallen on your face too many times today. Stop doing that.* It has to be because I'm tired. *I wouldn't be falling this much if I were fresh.* I try to encourage myself.

These burn sections in the Pasayten Wilderness are massive. The devastation just keeps going. The trees talk to you with their crackling as they move with the wind whistling between their bare, lifeless trunks. *It's like the souls of these dead trees are screaming.*

All of a sudden, I see a moose up ahead. I pause to admire her beauty. She pauses and stares back at me for a moment, then jets off and disappears into the dead forest. My first impression: She is much better at getting over these blowdowns than I am.

The ground has become dusty. The air is dry. I'm getting closer to the high deserts of Eastern Washington. I first noticed the change in climate between North Cascades National Park and Ross Lake. The national park was fertile and wet enough for mushrooms and moss everywhere. The west side of Ross Lake had slightly less moisture. Around on the east side of the lake you could tell the ground was slowly drying up, but the forests were still vibrant and full of life. Now that I'm in the Central Pasayten, I can feel the desert creeping in. Grass is no longer green. The vegetation is thinner and thirsty. It's fascinating to see such major changes in climate in just a couple of days' time by foot.

The clouds overhead part and the sun comes out in the afternoon, but this nice steady breeze that's been whistling through the trees is keeping everything cool. I begin to see evidence of freshly groomed trails. Fresh sawdust is on the ground; wind-snapped trees are cleared from the path. Being able to simply move forward without crawling under or climbing over a barricade from Mother Earth is such a relief.

Just as I begin climbing up the base of Bunker Hill, I come across the Pacific Northwest Trail Association (PNTA) maintenance crew. They are clearing the trails! I thank them for their work; the last couple of miles were joyful, easy-moving.

"Well, you're about to be back in it. We've only worked up to here so far," one of the guys spats.

"How bad is it?" I ask.

"Oh, you're f***ed," he responds back without hesitation.

I laugh, "Thank you for your honesty."

One of the girls in the trail crew contends, "It's only bad for a little bit longer. Once you get up in the alpine it's not so bad."

I thank them for their work again and continue on up the mountain. *I wish I had more time. It would be fun to pick up a saw and help them clear a few trees.*

Off topic, but I might be getting an ear infection. My inner ear pain has been getting worse all day. It's strange. I never have ear infections. *Maybe my body is just getting tired and not fighting off illness like it usually does?*

The blowdowns aren't as bad as I envisioned based on the description the PNTA trail crew gave me. Most are low to the ground and easy to get over, but eventually the trail becomes hard to follow. It's as if the trail was erased by the fire that came through here years ago. There's so much erosion, burn, and new plant growth the trail has almost disappeared. *This trail would be nearly impossible to follow in the dark.* Luckily, other hikers have stacked small cairns every now and then to help navigate through the miles of mountainside burn fields, and I'm thankful. Either way, this would still be absolutely miserable to navigate in the dark, and the sun is about to set. *I'll just keep going until I can't see the trail anymore.* But at the same time, I know I shouldn't camp in a burn field full of dead trees that could fall at any time—sleeping amongst widowmakers is not the brightest idea.

Just keep moving.

I come up to a meadow where a creek should be, but it's all dried up. I'm so disappointed. So thirsty. The last few comments on Guthooks mentioned a small amount of flowing water here, but it has all since shriveled away. *I was really looking forward to that stream.* Keep moving.

Just as I'm about to lose enough light to be able to navigate these eroded, trail-erased burn fields, I reach the alpine, and the trail becomes easy to follow. *Perfect timing. Again.*

The views on the way up and on top of Bunker Hill are mesmerizing—a 360-degree view of the Cascades in all directions. *Oh, how I'd love to bring Hannah here. Just spend a whole day up here soaking in these views.* The Cascades have a presence to them unlike any other mountain range I've been in. They have their own personality. I wish I had the time to stop here and watch the sunset, but I have to make it down this mountain and up the next before I can stop for the night. And then, as I'm coming back down the other side of the mountain, I find a flowing creek. From bloody cut-up legs and hundreds of blowdowns—to amazing views, easy-to-follow trails, and tasty cold mountain streams. The day is ending on a good note.

After the sun sets and the stars come out, the wind picks up speed. The temperature plummets. I bundle up with both my puffy and rain jacket, pull the hoods over my head, and cinch them down around my face. *I've reached the top of the next mountain. It's time to set up camp.* I check my map for potential campsite locations. The Barker Brown Cabin is just a few more miles ahead. Notes on Guthooks indicate it no longer has a roof. *But the walls will provide some solid wind protection.* I set out for the cabin.

A low cloud of fog rolls in. When I reach the area where the cabin should be, I can't see it. *It's somewhere near here off-trail, but in the dark and in this fog?* It would take too long to find. I start searching for a flat spot between some trees to have some kind of a wind barrier.

By the time I set up camp, it's 10:17 p.m., and I'm at mile 575.4. Through all those blowdowns, it still somehow managed to be a 48-mile day. *Maybe I'm capable of more than I thought.*

BOOKIN' IT

TODAY I'M NOT MOVING down the trail till 5:00 a.m. I'm moving slow from yesterday's beating. Owls hooting in the forest before sunrise seem to make up for it, though. I'll take an owl over a rooster any day.

A few hours into the morning, I approach a cabin, quite literally in the middle of nowhere. A mule is tied to the hitch outside.

"Hi there, Mr. Mule," I murmur.

A ranger comes around the corner of the cabin, off the wooden front porch, raises his cup of coffee and greets, "Good morning."

We have a brief conversation. He tells me about the heat wave that came through there earlier in the summer. It reached 137 degrees on his thermometer where he was patrolling one day. The wilderness just shriveled up in the heat—the trees, the streams, everything. It usually has a rush of lush green life in the late summer, but it never got the chance to come back this year.

"137 degrees. That's Death Valley temperatures!"

"Hotter than Death Valley."

My jaw drops. I can't even imagine. I feel like your insides would be cooking.

He asks for my permit.

"I need a permit out here?" I ask.

"Yes. You need a permit." He pauses and looks at me. "But you're headed east?"

"That's right."

"Most of you are headed west. The trailhead you came in on usually doesn't have a registry or way to obtain one. Here, I have one you can fill out in my bag." He goes inside for a moment, then returns with a permit tag and a pen.

Phew.

"Where did you start this morning?" he asks.

"I camped somewhere near the Barker Brown cabin."

"Hmmpff. You're bookin' it. How far are you headed tonight?"

"My goal is to get out of the Pasayten, to camp at the trailhead. That way I can say I've crossed the whole wilderness."

"OK, and when did you enter the Pasayten?"

"Friday night, just before sunset."

"So you're crossing the Pasayten in two days?"

"No, I allotted four days to get to Oroville from Ross Lake Resort… Oh wait, I guess that is, well, technically three days, two nights through the Pasayten.

"Friday night to Sunday night sounds like 48 hours to me. Just sayin'. And this is fun to you?"

We laugh. I fill out the rest of the tag, return a slip to him, and put my copy away. He offers for me to stay and have a cup of coffee with him, but I decline and explain that I really need to get to my miles.

The farther east I go, the drier everything becomes. I come upon Luden Lake, or what once was Luden Lake. It's nothing but a dry, empty flat pit now.

These Eastern Pasayten Wilderness trails are much easier to follow, much cleaner, and much more conducive to running. Everyone I've met on the PNT so far has been talking about how bad the Pasayten is. Yeah, the blowdowns are bad, but they didn't mention how easy the eastern side is. I've been making really good time despite being completely exhausted. Yesterday's blowdowns really wore me out.

A few hours later, I run into a couple of backpackers headed west, trail names Unruffled and Sound Effects. We chat for a minute, and then we get on our way. *One of these days I'll get a trail name of my own.*

I hear trampling hooves running through the woods. *Must be a herd of elk.* I pause, gazing through the trees, hoping to spot the mass of large game. Suddenly and surprisingly, about 25 cows running full speed come out of the trees and onto the open field. *Nope. Just cows.*

I make it out of the Pasayten before sunset and keep going. There's more time in the day, but as soon as darkness falls, so does my energy. I'm tired, ready to stop. I come across a Department of Natural Resources campground. *There's no one out here.* I walk past the first row of campsites and into a site in the middle of a patch of trees.

I lie down. The sky is clear. I'm happy it's not raining. I stare up at the stars as my body begins to relax. It aches, but it's a good ache. My feet. My legs. My hips. Pain with a side of endorphins. *I earned this.*

THE DESERT

UP AT 4:00 A.M. AGAIN. Today's a big day. I need to get to Oroville for a resupply and then back on trail, while still maintaining at least 45 trail miles. Resupplying always takes a chunk of time. Between picking up a resupply box, repacking, charging devices, and eating a big meal in town—it always seems to take at least a couple of hours. I also need to find some glue for my shoe; it's beginning to fall apart prematurely, and I'd rather nip it in the bud before it gets any worse. I still have several hundred more miles before I pick up my next pair. Plus, I need to find a pharmacy and get something for my ear. This ear infection seems to be getting worse. *Just keep it subsided until I make it to a pharmacy.*

As I pace down the trail, I check the map, but my GPS isn't working. Guthooks and Google Maps are showing I'm 100 miles south of where I'm actually at. My Garmin devices can't even find a satellite to connect with. I reset the networking settings on my phone, turn it off and back on, and try a few other tricks, but nothing seems to get the GPS to function properly.

I know I need to take a turn at some point, but I'm not sure which turn it is. More junctions are out here than appear on my map, and of course they aren't marked for the PNT. I keep moving east while counting junctions on the map and guesstimating the mileage. I end up having to use old-fashioned map and compass skills for a couple of hours before my GPS starts working again.

That GPS will spoil you.

Some people are sunset lovers, but I'm more of a sunrise guy. And I haven't seen a good one out here yet, until now—it's the first colorful sunrise of the entire trip. Maybe it was all the rain clouds and overcast skies blocking the sunrises before now? Or now that I'm in the high deserts of Eastern Washington and it's no longer raining I get an unobstructed view of the sun coming up? Could it be that I'm far enough away from the ocean that the horizon hues have changed? It has to have something to do with moisture or lack thereof. Sunsets and sunrises are always amazing in the desert.

Fortunately, the route toward Oroville is mostly downhill, easy cruising. My pack is nearly empty of food; it feels weightless. I'm making great time. I run for over 20 miles before slowing to a walk. *Twenty-five miles in before 10:00 a.m.!* I'm over halfway done with today's mileage, and it's not even noon. My legs are fresh. My feet aren't screaming. *Nothing can stop me!*

I come up to the backside of two temporary road barriers. I walk around and read the signs on them: "This area CLOSED. This includes trails and facilities until further notice." "Due to extreme fire danger, this area is CLOSED TO ENTRY." I never saw any trail closure signs when I entered. Maybe this is where PNT hikers are allowed to hike through, just not stop?

I make it to a paved road. I'll be on paved roads until I get to the other side of Oroville. I'm not excited about it; my feet are nervous—they were nearly beaten to death on the asphalt crossing the Puget Sound. A dog runs out from a farmyard and starts barking and following me. About a mile later he stops barking and just wags his tail as he runs around. I've made a new friend. Every once in a while, he stops to sniff something and then sprints toward me at full speed to catch up. *How long is this dog going to follow me?* A few miles later, an old farm truck drives up behind me and pulls over. The passenger jumps out, grabs the dog by the collar, and leads it to the bed of the truck. My new friend is gone—the only hiking buddy I've had for any length of distance on the PNT so far.

I start to pass by a house on Palmer Lake. A man is shoveling a pile of gravel from his driveway into a wheelbarrow. He sees me passing by his house, stops shoveling, and shouts, "Hang on! I'll get you a bottle of water!" *Must be a trail angel.*

While I'm waiting for him to return with water I want to return the favor, so I start shoveling the gravel into the wheelbarrow for him. He yells at me to stop and tells me to sit down at his picnic table in the shade overlooking the lake. He brings me a cold water bottle, a banana, and some string cheese. *DE-LI-CIOUS.* Cheese is one of nature's greatest gifts to humanity. *God bless bacteria.*

I thank him for the snacks and tell him how much I love his lakefront property. He proceeds to tell me how he and his wife retired there. One of their favorite features is that there's no cell phone service. "We can't stand cell phones. Everyone is always glued to them," his wife chimes in. "Out here we can be at peace and actually live in the moment."

I like that thought: "living in the moment." It's something I've been trying to get better at—my mind often finds itself focusing on the future. I thank them for their help and get back on my feet. I still have a ways to go before getting to Oroville.

The Similkameen River surprises me. The views make up for the pounding pavement. It's a canyon-carving river, cutting through tall rock walls and winding its way to and from Palmer Lake. Here's the interesting part: The trail angel I just met explained that this river can change its direction of flow. When Palmer Lake gets too full, the river will reverse and flow in the opposite direction.

I make it to Oroville close to 3:00 p.m., about an hour and a half earlier than I expect. I guess the road walks through the Puget Sound toughened up my feet because they didn't hurt nearly as bad this time.

This is the halfway point, at least by sign. Even if the numbers don't add up, it seems official. *Keep this pace and you'll be done in 28 days!* My chest puffs up. What is this? *That's the walk of confidence, Nick. You've got this.*

I grab my resupply box at the Camaray Hotel. *Why did I pack so much in this box? This is way too much to carry.* I pick and choose between what I decide to take with me. My overpacked resupply box is filled with tons of extra snacks and goodies to eat right here on the spot, but since I'm in town, I really just want a big hot meal at a restaurant.

Next, I'm at Pastime Brewery across the street. I start charging my devices and order an appetizer and brisket sandwich with a Dr Pepper. By the fourth refill, they bring me an entire pitcher. I finish the pitcher and get another Dr Pepper to go before leaving. (Yes, I am aware I have a problem.)

I head out to finish my town errands before getting back on trail. I pick up the strongest superglue I can find at the grocery store. *This had better hold.* It's hard to imagine a four-dollar glue holding a shoe together that's being pounded on for 45 miles a day.

Last stop on the way out of town, the pharmacy. But they are closed. *How awesome.* It's Labor Day. I suppose I could check the grocery store for ear drops. But no, I'm not backtracking toward the grocery store. I've been in Oroville for way too long as it is already; I need to get back on trail. *Meh, my ear isn't hurting too bad right now anyway.* Keep moving.

It's 5:00 p.m. The sun beats down on me from above while it reflects off the asphalt below at the same time. *Oh, holy mother of Abraham it's hot.* I'm sure it doesn't help that I just picked up six days' worth of food, the longest food carry of the entire trip.

I'm only allowing myself to resupply at locations the trail actually goes through—that way I never have to go out of my way, adding miles, for a resupply. The original plan was to resupply at Lake Bonaparte Resort, so I'd never be carrying more than five days of food at a time, but that option was thrown out the window when Mount Bonaparte caught fire a couple of weeks ago. Luckily, the fire isn't as bad anymore. It's contained. The fire crews are just waiting for it to finish burning out. Even though the fire is under control and no longer a threat, I still smell the smoke all the way here in Oroville, 40 miles away.

The good news is that the PNTA has a decent reroute listed to get around the fire closure. It's several miles longer than the original route, but it's doable. The only kicker is that I can't resupply at Lake Bonaparte

Resort anymore. I have to make it six days till my next resupply to make sure I'm not going dozens of miles out of the way. *Other than a few extra miles, what's just one more day's worth of food to carry?* That one more day of food is freaking heavy, is what it is.

As I'm walking down the shoulder of the highway out of Oroville, toward the Whistler Canyon trailhead, the waitress that served me at Pastime Brewery drives by. She pulls over, backs up, and asks if I want a ride to the trailhead.

Oh, how I would love a ride. It's scorching hot. My bag is heavy. I thank her but politely decline. "No, thank you. I appreciate it though." A few minutes later, a guy in a Camaro pulls over to offer me a ride. He's drinking a White Claw. "No, thank you."

My Snickers bar is no longer a Snickers bar. It's chocolate milk with some peanut chunks. It's liquid goo flopping around in a plastic wrapper. *This better not bust open and get all over everything. Actually, I'll make sure of that.* I carefully open the package and drink the contents. Then, I fold up the wrapper and tuck it away in a Ziploc to prevent the melted chocolate remnants from oozing into my pocket. I check the temperature: 89 degrees. *Yuck.*

I only make it a quarter mile up the Whistler Canyon trail, with my fully loaded bag, before stopping for a break in the only shady spot I've seen all afternoon. This heat is destroying me. I worked so hard to get here at this pace, and out of all these obstacles, this stupid heat is what's slowing me down. *It's not even 90 degrees. What is wrong with me?*

A day hiker walks past me, headed down the mountain in pants.

"I don't know how you're wearing pants in this heat!" I shout.

He comes over, "Oh, it was kinda chilly when I started this morning. I'll have 27 miles in by the time I get to the parking lot. I went all the way up to Summit Lake and back. How far are you going?"

"I'll probably make it 5–10 miles up this mountain. I'd really like to get to the top, but I don't know if I will with this heat." He sounded super proud of his 27 miles. I didn't have it in my heart to say, "I'm on mile 40 for the day, just going another 5–10 miles." Besides that, this guy can hike in this heat in full-length pants. That feat alone deserves respect. I certainly wouldn't do that. If all I had was pants, I'd be naked.

As I'm working my way up Whistler Canyon, I check the notes on Guthooks. I realize I've passed the last good water source until the other side of the mountain. As much as I hate to backtrack, I drop my pack, grab my water bottles, and run back down the mountain for water. *My bag better still be there when I get back.* I start considering the risks of leaving a bag with six days worth of food alone in the middle of a desert forest trail.

The run back down the mountain is effortless and quick. It's no longer exhausting to move. *Is it the heat, or is it the weight of six days of food on my back?* It's both, but taking one of those elements out of the equation makes all the difference in the world.

I get my water, return to my bag, and keep climbing on up. It's cooled off significantly by now. I've traded the blazing heat with the weightlessness of no bag, back to a heavy bag without the heat. *The sun will be down soon.* I start hustling. If I can get out of this canyon and up to the ridge, I'll be able to catch the sun setting over the Pasayten Wilderness.

As soon as the trail flattens out on top, the canyon hills drop and slowly invert into cliffside bluffs. The view to the west, toward the Pasayten Wilderness, extends past three separate layers of mountains, each one slightly taller than the other. I've caught the tail end of the sunset. Golden and blue hues paint the landscape.

Looking out over the Western Cascades is comforting and encouraging. *I just crossed all that, the whole Pasayten Wilderness, in 48 hours.* I laugh to myself thinking about the ranger I had met the previous morning.

Not even fifteen minutes later, I decide to call it a night. There's a small flat spot next to a picnic table on top of the bluff, with the same sunset view over the Pasayten. Super random spot for a picnic table—I wonder who had to bring it all the way up here. I claim the table as my prep station, lay out all my sweaty, wet clothes to dry, and begin gluing the toe of my shoe back together. *I can't believe I'm actually sitting down watching the sunset. What a treat.* This gives me enough time to make sure the glue dries overnight before I get moving again in the morning. Plus, I've already done 45 miles today and picked up a resupply—that's a lot for a day—especially with how hot it's been. I wedge some rocks against my shoe to hold the glue in place overnight and get to bed.

COW PATTIES

UP AT 4:00 A.M. Today's mission is to get around the Mount Bonaparte fire. Also, eat as much food as possible to make this pack lighter.

As I grab the clothes I laid out on the picnic table last night, I'm amazed. Everything is completely dry. *It's so dry here; my clothes even dried without the sun.* Usually, my shirt is still sopping wet in the morning.

After strolling through a few mountain trails, I end up on a dirt forest service road. I start to pass a wooden cabin with several "no trespassing" signs. Despite the signs, I find myself looking for a water spigot on the side of it as I walk by. Then I notice a porta-potty in the yard. *It must be an off-grid cabin with no running water.*

Thirsty. I have a quarter of a liter of water left, and it needs to last another eight miles. Eight more miles in this hot, dry, thirst-starved forest. I'm officially in the high deserts of Eastern Washington, and I'm certainly feeling the lack of water sources. Everything is dried up out here.

I start passing by more cabins. The cabins slowly turn into trailers, and the yards start filling up with random items. Eventually, the yards are scattered with mobile homes, old travel trailers, and broken-down paint-faded cars. One lot has nearly half a dozen mobile homes on it. Some of the trailers have blue tarps tied down over the roofs. Couches are outside. Rusted out 50-gallon drums. Decks built out from the travel trailers. Wheelbarrows. Propane bottles. Stacked firewood. I see smoke coming out of a wood stove pipe sticking out the roof of a 5th wheel travel trailer. *These aren't mountain getaway cabins anymore. These are communes.* A plethora of "no trespassing" signs decorate the trees, fences, and gates. Dogs on chains bark viciously at me. I consider asking one of these friendly folk for some water, but that thought doesn't last long. *Just keep moving.*

Right about this time, my mom's husband Mark texts me. I tell him about the water situation, and he tells me he'll pray that I find a water source earlier than the eight miles. Fifteen minutes later, I come across water flowing through a culvert under the road. I'm thankful. I crawl into the ditch to fill my bottles and then smell the aroma coming from the source. *Is that sewage?* It's revolting. But it's clear. And flowing. *It can't be that bad.*

I guess this is where we find out how thirsty I am. I have a filter. That should do the trick, right? I filter a third of a liter and get on my way. *I'll just take enough to get me to the next source. I'll only drink it if I have to.*

A few miles later, I take a sip of my fresh "filtered water." The taste is pungent. I check the map again for water sources—there don't appear to be any for quite a while. I add an electrolyte mix in an attempt to mask the acridity and take a sip. *Elgch. Yuck. This is awful.*

The smell of smoke grows stronger. Plumes of gray loft up, creating a halo over Mount Bonaparte. Now's time to start the fire reroute. It's 28 miles long, and it's all road walk. *Gross.* I'm looking forward to getting this day of mostly paved roads out of the way.

I stumble across a sign for the "Havillah Church Trail Angels." It's directing PNT hikers to the church less than a third of a mile away. The sign indicates hikers can use their bathroom, fill water bottles, and even camp in their yard if needed. *Score!* I pour out my nasty, emergency-only water.

As I approach the white-steepled building, I notice more signs for PNT hikers—and finally catch sight of the flames on Mount Bonaparte, situated on the far side of a field behind the church. No one is here, but the directions illustrate hikers are welcome to go inside on their own.

The door is unlocked. I give myself a quick tour; it's a small church. It's exciting to explore and check out the stained glass windows. The kitchen has signs directing hikers to boxes of Gatorade and food they are welcome to. Frozen dinners are in the freezer labeled for hikers. *They even have food we can eat? Get out of here!* This would be a great place to spend more time if I had it. I tell myself I won't stay longer than 15 minutes.

I flush my bottle out, hoping none of the stifling smells have soaked into the plastic. I start cooking a pot pie, drink a Gatorade, and use the bathroom. Toilet paper and running water. *Luxury.*

OK, I've been here too long already. I need to get moving. As I scarf down the chicken pot pie, I leave a few of my food items behind to replace what I take and get back on the road. I have nearly 30 miles to go on this detour, and I'm determined to finish it and get back on trail today.

A few hours later, I'm at the Chesaw Tavern. I order chicken and fries to go. I've already spent too much time not moving today. As I'm leaving, a delivery guy walks through the front door. He claims he saw me walking down the road near Havillah, "You move fast!"

"I'm on a mission," I respond.

"A mission? Let me tell you about some of my missions." He walks outside with me and tells me tales of when he was fighting for the Spanish Legion in Afghanistan. Ambush stories, saving families that were being slaughtered, setting up traps in the mountains. *This is one hard-core guy.* He grabs a couple of Gatorades from his delivery truck and gives them to me. "Here, you need these more than I do."

"Thank you!" *He's generous too.*

A couple of hours and about eight more miles go by. The road goes downhill through Beaver Canyon and passes by a few lakes. The warm meal gives me a boost. It's easy to make good time. I come across a rope swing hanging from a tree leaning over one of the lakes. Oh, how I would love to swing and jump in the water, but I'm too tired to climb back up the steep embankment to get out afterward. Besides that, I just don't feel like dealing with being wet right now. I'm finally dry.

I haven't had to deal with rain or wet bushes in a couple of days. I'd rather stay this way. *I bet the water does feel nice, though.* Sitting down in the shade of the tree, I stare at the rope swing and take a break for five minutes. I imagine swinging from the rope and splashing in the cool, refreshing lake below. First a backflip, then a cannon ball and a gainer. I'm more capable in my imagination than I am in real life.

Keep moving.

Between the church, tavern, delivery guy, and the beautiful lakes in this canyon—this detour isn't turning out to be so bad. I originally thought today was going to be nothing but hot and miserable on these paved roads of Eastern Washington.

At the end of the lakes I see a beaver dam. *Ha. I guess that's why it's called Beaver Canyon.* The enticing canyon walls slowly fade. By the time the lakes disappear I start to pay closer attention to the trash on the sides of the road.

Want to know what kind of trash I see out here the most? Beer cans, White Claws, and Twisted Teas. Know what that means? A bunch of people drink and drive and then throw their evidence out the window here. *Beer can, beer can, Twisted Tea, beer can. Oh, wait, that's an empty chocolate milk bottle. Maybe that guy was just having breakfast.*

My step has lost its pep. Trails give me energy; pavement takes it away. It's mundane. *Only six more miles of road.* I start entertaining myself more so than usual. I sing about how tired I am of road walks. As I'm walking past some cows, I happen to be eating a piece of beef jerky. "I'm eatin' your cousin. I'm eatin' your cousin!" I sing to the cows and wave my jerky as I walk by.

Next I come across a handful of abandoned log cabins next to the road. Decrepit and falling apart, most have signs that read, "No Trespassing." *But this one doesn't have a sign.* I don't even try to fight the urge to explore. I deserve something after having to be on these paved roads for so many miles. I sneak in through the front door of the only two-story wooden structure. The floor is half caved-in and broken. All the windows are shattered. I can see upstairs through the ceiling that's falling apart. Boards creak underneath my feet. I make it about 20 steps inside before stopping. *Nope. Not worth it.* It'd be a blast to explore, but if my leg broke through one of these boards and I hurt myself, it would make the rest of this trip tougher than it has to be.

Keep moving.

Next up: more sketchy cabins, trailers, and debris-filled yards. Completely trashed, vandalized cars are abandoned on the sides of the dirt road. Hateful messages (not worth repeating) are even graffitied onto said cars. *I don't even want to know how that car got a crater-sized hole in its windshield.* Signs are everywhere, making it evident no one is welcome. They clearly don't want visitors.

Before the sun goes down, I'm back on foot trails. The fire reroute is done. I've completed today's miles. I look up with thanksgiving—just a few puffy clouds dot the cerulean sky. *I've already done 45 miles, and it's still light out!*

This morning I planned to camp at the first available spot once I got back on trail, but it's Hannah's birthday today. I haven't had cell service, so I haven't called her yet. I check the map. *If there's service anywhere out here, it's on top of Clackamas Mountain.*

Onward I go, climbing in elevation toward the top. *Bear print!* I take a picture of it next to my size 12 foot for comparison. It makes my foot look small. From paved roads to wilderness with bear prints in just a handful of miles. A smile takes over my face. I'm back in my happy place. I'm back in the woods.

My pace quickens. The timing could be right. *If I make it to the top before the end of the hour, I could catch the sunset with a good view.* Even though I'm back in shaded forest trails and the sun is beginning to go down, I'm sweating profusely. I keep wiping my forehead with my shirt and chant to myself. *Just two more miles. Just two more miles.*

My shorts start to get wet with sweat. *Ugh. That's just going to make the chafing worse.* I haven't seen another hiker since yesterday. *Screw it.* I take my shorts off. It's a double win. Prevents chafing and keeps the shorts dry.

I'm hiking naked... again.

I'm glad I'm the only one out here. Thank goodness this is the PNT and not the PCT. I don't know how I would ever be able to stop the chafing on the PCT. That trail has so much traffic; I'd never be able to get away with something like this.

Just before I make it to the highest point of the trail on Clackamas Mountain, I can tell the sunset is almost over. It'll be gone in a couple of minutes—and I haven't had a chance to appreciate it yet. I jet off-trail when I see a small ridge to climb up for a good view. The very end of the sunset is disappearing behind Mount Bonaparte. The sun itself is already gone; it's only the afterglow that remains. The silhouette of the smoke from the fire is rising up and drifting its way through the last bits of orange left on the horizon. I never thought a mountain on fire could be so beautiful.

When I get to the top of Clackamas, I have one bar of cell service. Not 4g, not 3g, just one bar of nothing. I try calling. I try texting. I try standing up on top of the tallest rock I can find while holding my phone as high up in the air as possible. Nothing will go through. *Dear Verizon, "No, I cannot hear you now."*

And then I realize I can just text Hannah from the InReach. Not only is my InReach tracking my whole trip for FKT purposes, it also gives me the ability to text from anywhere via satellite. I had completely forgotten about that ability since I stopped using the InReach texts to save battery. I send her a message. It's nearly 10:00 p.m. here. That means it's almost midnight for her. She's probably already asleep. *Oops.*

I start searching for a flat spot to lie down for the night. Cow patties are everywhere. I walk off-trail to the left, toward a flat spot. It's covered in cow patties. I walk off-trail to the right and soon find another flat spot. But it's covered in cow patties too. I keep moving forward. Cow patties. I go backward a little. Cow patties.

My body is beyond exhausted, and I've already mentally checked into the idea of lying down for the night. I'm ready to be done. I've never been so frustrated by cow manure in my life. *How is there so much crap out here? Are these cows sick or something?*

I want to lie down so bad. I just don't want to lie down in cow dung. *Keep moving.*

Ten minutes later, I find a somewhat flat spot in the middle of the trail. It looks clean; I don't see any patties. It's on a slight slope, but it's not too bad. *Meh, I can just lie with my legs uphill again. It'll be good to keep them elevated.* After laying out my bivy, I spot an old, white, crispy patty just inches away. I look around the perimeter of where I'll be lying. I see a couple more out-dated crispies. *At least I'm not ON cow patties.*

I lie down on top of my bivy and start rubbing my feet. Big red ants crawl over the foot box of my quilt. I shine my light to the side. A dirt volcano is forming an ant hill less than two feet away. I shake the ants off, wipe my quilt with my hands, and then slide inside my bivy and zip up to be enclosed.

I check the map. I'm at mile 713 exactly. A 51.1-mile day. *Can't believe I finally broke 50 miles.* I've done several 49-mile days on the PNT so far, but this is the first time to officially go over 50. That motivation to talk to Hannah is what got me here—Hannah is the one who got me past that 50-mile mark.

SKINNY DIPPING

MY STOMACH RUMBLES. The first thought on my mind when I open my eyes is food. That, and I'm exhausted. I slept hard, but I don't feel rejuvenated. My arms quiver as I pack my bag—not because it's cold, but because I'm weak. In fact, it's warm. I'm not even hiking yet, and I don't need my jacket. I try not to think about the heat that'll be beating down this afternoon.

A few more unmarked trail junctions come up. Guthooks doesn't even list them. I'm thankful I have my other map. This isn't the first time I've been thankful to have it either.

No freaking way! A light sprinkle begins to cool the air off. I look up, nothing but clouds. Today might not be so bad after all.

I come across a few cows on the trail. They become startled and sprint up the hillside to get away from me. *These mountain cows are agile!* I'm pretty sure they're climbing faster than I would.

It turns out the three-minute sprinkle fest this morning was just a tease. The clouds are gone. The sun is out in full force—and it's hot. It's barely even 8:00 a.m.

As I come to my first water source for the day, I take my bag off for a break. The next reliable source is 20 miles away. And with this heat, I know I'm going to need all the fluids I can get. In an effort to not have to carry as much weight, I chug two liters of water and carry three.

There is NO ONE out here. Trails are vacant. Haven't seen any hikers in a couple of days now. Maybe everyone is still skipping this part of the trail and hitching over to Oroville to avoid the Mount Bonaparte fire? *It's going to be a chafe-free day today!* Might as well hike naked while I can.

I loop the liner of my shorts through one of the sternum straps on my backpack, so they hang down and at least cover me up from the front. *Dual purpose.* It's like I'm hanging up my shorts to dry, which are already wet with sweat from the heat of the morning, but I get to maintain some form of decency in the slim chance I come across another human out here.

OK, cameling up and drinking two liters of water is slowing me down. I'm stopping to pee every 30 minutes. However, it's crystal clear. I laugh to myself. *Watch the desert sections end up being where I'm the most hydrated.* Best part about it though? I don't even have to pull my pants down—I'm free as a bird.

The trail has been following an old forest service road through the mountain for a while. I hear a truck coming from around the corner at the last minute. I unbuckle my sternum strap, grab my shorts, and put them on faster than I've ever put shorts on in my life. I'm talking naked to clothed in less than three seconds. The pickup rolls around the corner just as I'm finishing. *Was I fast enough?* I think so. But the guy driving this truck must have seen me on the tail end of the short-slip shuffle. He's probably thinking, "What in the world is this guy doing out here?"

A couple of hours later, I sit down to take a rock out of my shoe. It takes me two minutes just to stand back up. *I'm stiff.*

Next, I drop my bag and go off-trail to do my business. It feels like I'm floating. I'm so light. I feel like I could fly if I didn't have to carry a pack. *I probably shouldn't have just left my pack in the middle of the trail.*

Ah, yes. I love it when I get somewhere an hour earlier than planned. I've made it to my first bushwhack of the day. A handful of rocks stacked next to the forest service road look like the workings of a fellow PNT hiker. A much larger cairn, piled twenty or so steps off to the side, must have been built by the PNTA as an official marker. It's indicating the beginning of the bushwhack, which doesn't look too bad. Since it's so dry out here, it doesn't appear that many bushes have had a chance to grow to an annoying size. It should be fairly easy to navigate for not having a trail.

"Bushwhacking! Here I come!" I shout to the woods and march forward.

The blowdowns are small, easy to get over. For a while I feel like I'm following somewhat of a social trail or game trail, but eventually I don't see anything that resembles a trail at all. I pull my phone out and follow the GPS dot on the screen. *If I just go this way, I should eventually see something.* Keep moving.

The dry, dead, prickly vegetation grows thicker. Waist-to-elbow-high plants with what looks like fluffy white cotton start to take over the landscape. As I forge my way through the fields of thick-stemmed, grass-like weeds, I quickly discover the cotton fluffs are sticky. It clings to my legs and shorts. It looks like I've been tarred and feathered.

Soon I come across a clearing. *There's a trail out here?* It's fresh. Cleanly cut.

I hear a voice, "The trail's a lot easier moving forward from here."

When I look up I see three members of the PNTA trail crew about 50 feet away. They've been carving a path through the bushwhack.

I sit down on a log and chat with them for a few minutes. A rush of relaxation courses through my body; gravity is no longer working against my legs. Matthew, Sarah, and Greg have been out here cleaning up trails all summer it seems. Right now, actually forming a path where there was no path before. They advise of a few other areas they did some work on in the previous weeks. I'm ever so thankful for their work! It turns out one of them, Matthew, met Joe "Stringbean" McConaughy on the Arizona Trail when Joe was setting the FKT on it earlier this year. "And now I've met you." Matthew asks if I've ever hiked the Appalachian Trail.

"No."

"Continental Divide Trail? Arizona Trail?"

"No."

"Is this your first thru-hike?"

"Yeah."

"You're doing over 40 miles a day and going for an FKT on your first thru-hike?!"

"I suppose so."

I thank them for their work and try to stand back up. But I don't make it all the way and end up sitting back down. The trail crew and I laugh. I stand up on the second attempt and start shuffling down the trail. Greg says, "Oh! I thought we broke him." Matthew then shouts, "Hey, go for a swim in the lake up ahead! It's a great swim spot. It'll cool you down and make you 25% faster."

It's miserably hot. I'm covered in sticky cotton fluffs. A swim would be nice. I haven't had a shower or any form of bathing in 500 miles. *Maybe that's why Matthew suggested the swim. I'm awfully ripe.*

My nose starts to bleed. *Great.* I lean my head back and plug my nose, trying to keep it manageable so it doesn't slow me down too much.

Once I make it to Swan Lake, I see a sign warning hikers: "Monkshood - Do Not Eat or Touch!" Monkshood is a deadly plant that can cause paralysis if it touches a mucus membrane on the human body and can even be fatal if consumed. It's described as "generally produces a stout, unbranched stem rising three to six feet high." *Ummmm. That sounds like the cottony plants I just walked through.* I keep reading. *Ah, this poisonous plant has a flower often shaped like a "hood."* I don't remember any flowers. *What if this is the off-season? The flower comes in the spring and this cottony mess is in the fall?* I mean, after all, this trail does seem to intentionally go through all the nasty vegetation. Stinging nettle, then a bushwhack through blackberry brambles, thousands of blowdowns—now monkshood? Sounds about right.

There's a picnic table near the swimming beach. I don't see anyone. *I'll just jump in and out. Just a rinse.* I strip my clothes, leave everything on the picnic table, run into the water and dive in. It's refreshing. Rejuvenating. I scrub my body briefly, trying to take advantage of the chance to get clean, before swimming underwater on my way out.

I shake off like a dog and slip back into my clothes. Thirty seconds later an older couple walk around the corner without even carrying daypacks. *There must be a parking lot over there.* I'm glad they didn't show up two minutes sooner. I refill my water bottles, and I'm on my way.

Hours and miles go by. Up and down, over and around. There is a trail; there's not a trail. I'm on a road; now I'm not.

I pick up enough water for the next 30 miles—the biggest water carry of the entire trip. I chug two liters and carry five. This area is already naturally dry with minimal water sources. Adding in the fact that I'm going through here late in the season means there's practically no natural water left at all. *And it's hot. It's so freaking hot.*

The sun has set, but there's still a slight natural glow on the horizon, lingering on for as long as it can. I hear a rattlesnake. It's about a foot off the trail on the left side up ahead. It's small, but it's pretty pissed off. The small snakes can be more dangerous than the bigger ones. The younger they are, the less control they have over how much venom they release. It's coiled up, head raised, tail rattling like crazy. It's ready to strike.

I step off the trail to the right to work my way around it while keeping a safe distance. I know some people, mainly my mom, are freaked out that I'm running through bear country in the middle of the dark on this trip, but I'm not worried about the bears. In all reality, this, the rattlesnake is likely the biggest danger I'll encounter. You can hear a bear from a distance. They usually hear or see you first and run away before you can even get a good look. Bears are smart; they don't want to mess with a human. I'm not even planning on carrying bear spray or any form of bear protection until I get into grizzly country in Idaho and Montana. But a rattlesnake could just lie there in the middle of the trail, camouflaged and hidden. You could end up stepping on it because you didn't see it in the dark.

Not today, snake.

I keep moving.

A couple of hours later, I reach a flat spot near mile 753. It's only a 39.9-mile day. *Not even 40 miles.* I haven't made it as far as I want to go, but I need to stop. Today's been hard. Lots of bushwhacking. Heavy water carries. The heat. I'm glad it's over.

WIDOWMAKERS

MY BATTERY BANK DIED last night. Phone is at 70%. InReach is at 39%. I have to somehow make this last three more days till I can get to Northport and charge up.

Before the sun is up, I'm climbing over more blowdowns.

Lots more blowdowns.

I'm absolutely exhausted, and the day has just begun. I'm surprised there's still a smokey haze and smell in the sky despite being two days away from the Mount Bonaparte fire. *This part of the trail must be downwind—or—there's another fire.*

The trees darken. They are alive, but they look as if they had been burned in a fire a long time ago. The closer I get to them, the more I realize they aren't burnt at all; their bark is just black. The trees are skinny, tall, and close together. They actually have some green to them. *This is the healthiest-looking forest I've seen since the Pasayten.*

Miles later I'm cursing the woods as I go through the bushwhack up Edd's Mountain. The forest isn't as lively. It's miserably hot. It's a steep climb. It's noon—the sun is directly overhead. Some of this area was clearly in a wildfire a long time ago; some of it looks like a tinderbox just waiting to go up in flames. There's no shade whatsoever. Dead trees are all clumped together. Some standing, seems like half are blown over. There must be thousands of blowdowns out here. They're all small trees, maybe only 8–10 inches in diameter, but it's the constant high steps to get over them that are wearing me out. I check my GPS. I've gone way off track from where the map indicates to go through the bushwhack. *I'll just cut straight across to reconnect with the line.*

I'm drained. My legs are heavy. I keep cutting my legs on blown-down tree limbs. I'm tripping and falling, over and over again. Sweat beads up on my skin. It saturates my clothes. Debris from squeezing between trees and bushes sticks to my arms and my legs. It falls down my shirt collar and irritates the back of my neck. It's taxing. Infuriating. It takes me over an hour to go just a half-mile up the steep scramble littered with brush and debris. I'm on edge. It's sweltering. Blazing hot. Hotter than yesterday. I just want to cry. I scream into the woods.

Today sucks.

Once I make it to the top of the ridge and reconnect with the trail, I stop to take a break. I take my shirt off to wring the sweat out. Dark, murky water pours out like a faucet. I continue to wring it out several more times. Each time, more dirty brown fluid seeps out.

I turn my phone off airplane mode to see if I have cell service on top of the mountain. I want to call Hannah. She'll talk some sense into me—get my mind right. And there is service! Messages start flooding in. Some of them business-related. I'm tired, emotional, and pissed off. One of the messages is from a business partner asking me to send in an email to authorize a change on an account, something that wouldn't normally bother me, but I'm fuming. *I told them what I'm doing. They know I can't handle work right now. I'm not responding to that today.*

I'm able to reach Hannah on the phone. I can barely hold back the tears. She reminds me to focus on neutral thoughts. Don't hold on to the good, because it'll make the suck suck that much worse. Don't focus on the suck, because, it freaking sucks. Just focus on the neutral thoughts.

Neutral thoughts. Just think neutral thoughts.

I check the temperature now that I have cell service. *94 degrees. Ugh.*

I've been sweating a lot. I've been drinking water faster than I normally do; I'm almost out. I need to slow down to make sure my water lasts till I find another source.

Not too much later I come across a winter ski cabin, accessible to hikers during the off-season. I check it for water, but there's none. It's stocked with more food than I could have ever imagined, firewood, and even cots. But no water.

Keep moving.

Hannah texts me, "You're ahead of schedule overall. Why don't you stop early, just get in the minimum miles you need, and take a break today?"

"I'm not out here to do the minimum, Hannah." Despite my misery, my stubbornness persists.

I run out of water, and it's only getting hotter. Eventually I come across a cattle trough under a piped spring that's dripping every few seconds. The trough has been collecting that drip for quite some time; it's full to the brim. Floaties, bugs, and some pretty nasty-looking debris are in it. *Is that a dead mouse?* I try not to look at it, so I don't wonder how long it's been there or how contaminated the water is. *What are filters for?* I dunk my bottle, quickly fill it, and get on my way.

A few hours later, I'm on the Kettle Crest Trail and out of the burn area. The shade returns, and the temperatures cool off. I'm thankful.

I see bunnies hopping through the forest. Some run across the trail in front of me. They're everywhere. I've never seen so many rabbits before. *They've been busy.*

Hours later, I come across a piped spring sticking out the side of a steep embankment. *I suppose I should collect some of that.* I fill an eighth of a liter in two minutes. It's taking too long. Keep moving.

My InReach battery dies. *There goes my live tracker.* I'm nowhere near Northport, the next town the trail goes through. I attempt to use cell service to find out my options, but the signal is weak, causing my battery to drain even faster as my phone searches for a stronger signal. My phone is down to 21%. Battery bank is already dead. I desperately need juice. I game plan to detour off-trail and go into Orient tomorrow. It'll add nearly eight miles round-trip to the hike. *Ugh.* I really hate to sidetrack like this, but if I get lost in another bushwhack my GPS makes it so much easier to get back on track. It could be crucial. Plus, I need the InReach tracking for FKT purposes.

A cow follows me on the trail for roughly two miles. At first from a distance, slowly gaining on me. Eventually it's less than five feet behind me. If I stop, it stops. Once I start moving, it starts moving too. "What are you doing, cow?" It just moos back at me. I walk backward on the trail to get a good look at it. I'm surprised it's been following me for so long. And then…

Trip and *THUMP.*

I trip on a limb and fall down. *Watch where you're going, Nick.* Could have called that. Walking backward close to dusk is just asking for a fall. Eventually I step off the trail and the cow runs by. *Finally.*

I'm relieved, but not for long. My stalker cow calls for reinforcements until there's an army of bovines kicking up dust in my face. If I keep a quick pace, I'm constantly in the plume. If I go slow, the dust settles momentarily before I catch back up with them. *Why won't they just get off the trail? Shouldn't have let her pass.*

An incredible sunset unfolds. The best one of the trip so far. It even pairs itself with a tiny sliver of the crescent moon. I can see Mount Bonaparte burning far off in the distance. Orange, yellow, and blue whisk the sky. The black silhouettes of trees form a wall up close, separating me from the vast open valleys below and the sun setting in the horizon. It's a beautiful ending to a rough day.

By the time the sun is gone, it's back to just me on the trail.

I see another forest fire up ahead, maybe 10 miles away. The flames are easy to spot in the dark. I'm not sure which fire this is, but it seems like I'm headed straight toward it. I check the map. *Yeah, I'm still headed the right way.* I check the fire alerts with my dying cell phone battery and don't see anything new I wasn't aware of. It must be that little fire on the east side of the Kettle Crest. *Shouldn't be a problem.*

I'm zapped. Moving slow. Thank goodness it's cooled off, but that heat earlier in the day really wiped me out.

Soon I'm back in another burn area. Dead trees stand everywhere, widowmakers. Some can fall without any warning. It's not safe to camp here. *I need to make it out of here, then I can sleep.*

Miles go by. I'm tired. I've been tired all day, but now I'm especially tired. I'm tripping over the smallest obstacles. I keep stepping and stumbling off the trail. By the time 10:00 p.m. hits I decide I need to go to sleep. *I won't be sleeping that long. What are the chances a tree is going to fall on me within six hours?*

A flat spot in the trail comes up. It's just long enough for me to lie down. Tall, dead trees loom all around. They creak and they sway in the wind. *Just six hours.* Out comes my bivy, and I'm lying down in the middle of the trail. I look up at the widowmakers towering over me. Sketchy. Not recommended at all. I check the map. Forty point one miles for the day.

OUT OF JUICE

MY HEADLAMP DIES SHORTLY after 4:00 a.m. as I pack up camp. *Thank goodness I brought a backup.* I swap out my headlamps. *Because I have no more power.*

After a couple of hours, the sun comes up allowing me to see smoke rising over a saddle and settling in the valley below. The smoke is so thick it looks like fog. *This can't be good for my lungs.*

My phone's battery is at 7%. That means no more pictures. No more videos. No more using it for anything until I get to town to charge up. There's still one more bushwhack between here and Orient, and I'm not sure how bad it is. If it's a mess, I'll need my GPS to get through it quicker. I hope it's nothing like what I went through yesterday.

The trail is mostly an easy-going downhill cruise all the way to town. I'm making great time. When I come across the bushwhack, I'm elated to find out it's not that difficult. A decent social trail is forming from all the other hikers this year. *Thank you.* My spirits begin to lift. I pick up the pace. It's much cooler today too. Dark clouds roll in overhead, blocking out the sun. *Thank you, thank you, thank you.*

Hannah did some reconnaissance for me last night to save my battery from internet searches. She told me there's a family diner in Orient. *Once I make it to the diner, I can sit down, relax, charge up my tech, and charge up my body.* I hustle, taking advantage of the clean trails. The faster I get to the diner, the more time I'll have to charge everything, and I know it's going to take a while since everything is completely dead.

I order the biggest breakfast meal they have: giant waffles, eggs, hash browns, bacon, and toast. I get a lemonade AND a Dr Pepper, with multiple refills of each.

I do the math—something I seem to be constantly doing in my head these days. I need to average slightly more than 45 miles a day from here on out to finish the trail in 28 days. *Wow. That's actually still doable.* I guess that's about what I've been averaging. I just have to keep the pace up—I can't have any more of these 40-mile days.

I stay at the diner for two hours. Besides the two people who were at the bar when I got here, I'm the only customer who has come in all morning. My electronics aren't all the way charged yet, but I can't stand to stay past 12 o'clock.

I swing by the general store, hoping to replace my water bottle. Mold keeps growing back in the lid. I've washed it out a few times, but it keeps coming back. *Why don't they have Smartwater bottles? Don't they realize Smartwater makes you smarter?* I want a bottle that's sturdy enough for long-term use, fits my pockets perfectly, and has threads that fit my water filter—but I don't see one. *What's another couple of days of mold?* I can replace it when I get to Northport or Metaline Falls.

Coming back out of Orient, the pressure drops. It feels like it's going to rain. *We will see.* I was teased with this same feeling a couple of days ago.

The clouds thicken, and the sky darkens. A light sprinkle begins. It's not heavy enough to need a rain jacket, but it is enough to increase my speed. My body doesn't have to cool itself anymore. *This is perfect. Stay right there.* I hope the rain doesn't get heavier for my sake, but at the same time I hope it does—this area needs it.

I end up meeting a county sheriff driving some of the forest service roads. *Why is there a cop out here?* He gives me a weather report: It's supposed to rain like this all night until tomorrow morning around 5:00 a.m. *Well, at least I know.* I haven't had good enough cell service to look up the weather, and with how desert-like it's been since Oroville,

I've been half expecting it to be dry all the way to Idaho. He gives me a piece of gum and offers me some water, but I politely decline. A stream follows the trail not too far ahead, and water is heavy. Over two pounds a liter heavy. I'm only carrying what I have to.

The officer is right. The rain doesn't let up. In fact, it gets heavier. Hours and hours pass. Once darkness falls, the temperature drops with it. I keep pushing toward a campsite on the map that's supposed to have a privy. It's five more miles than I planned to go for the night, but it's a chance to keep my gear dry while I pitch my tarp. I laugh at myself. *Look at me. Yesterday, miserably hot in the high deserts of Eastern Washington wishing it would cool off, and now I'm soaking wet and cold, wishing everything was dry.*

Eventually, I make it to the campground. As I'm searching for the bathroom I come across the first designated campsite. A dry, flat spot presents itself between two trees. I look around. It's the only dry spot I see, and it just so happens to be the perfect size.

I stop looking for the privy and set up camp under the trees. As soon as I'm lying down, the wind shifts and rain starts sprinkling on my paper-thin roof. *Just in time.*

I've just about nailed this nightly routine. It's starting to become habitual—and quick. I check the map. Forty-nine point four trail miles plus 7.4 miles in and out of Orient. *That's a 56.8-mile day!* And my feet don't hurt nearly as bad as I would have expected for such high mileage. Maybe my body is adapting. Maybe I'm just getting used to the pain.

FLANKED

IT'S STILL RAINING, which always makes taking down camp a little more tedious.

By 6:00 a.m., the rain turns into a thick fog. I'm thankful to be back in the fog instead of smoke, and I'm thankful the rain has stopped. My feet are atrocious. Yesterday's rain brought the trenchy, dark-pitted nastiness back to my feet, as if the several days of dry weather from Oroville to Orient never happened—as if I've been walking through rain this entire time.

Since I pushed to make it to that campground last night, I'm ahead of schedule. I cross the Columbia River bridge and make it to the Northport Shell gas station to pick up a few resupplies—primarily a new water bottle to replace my moldy lid one. I pull on the door. It's locked. They are still closed. The sign says they open in 20 minutes. No time to waste; keep moving.

I'm so sleepy this morning. Those 50-plus-mile days just wipe me out.

My shoulders are tired, tired of carrying the weight of this pack. I'm only one day from Metaline Falls, my next resupply town. My pack is fairly light. I've eaten the majority of the food I've been carrying. Why does it feel so heavy? Maybe it's the weight of the whole trip piling up on me.

I walk past a mailbox that has the words "FAT CAMP" on it. *You've got to be kidding me. There's no way there's a fat camp out here in the middle of nowhere. Are fat camps even real? Someone must have written this on their mailbox as a joke.*

Next, I come across a hiker box on the side of the road in some guy's yard. It's just one of those big black plastic tubs with a yellow lid sitting next to a tree, but it has a laminated sign on it: "PNT Hiker Box" with the PNT emblem.

I haven't seen another hiker in days. Heck, the last thru-hiker I saw was in the Pasayten Wilderness. I stop, open the lid, and check out what's inside. Bottles of water and travel-size tissue packs. I see a welcome note to PNT hikers: "Hikers: You are welcome to camp in my yard, use the outhouse, and even get in the shed for a dry place to bunker down if it's raining." I scan his property. Looks like he's living in a truck camper, has a porta-potty for a bathroom, and a small shed for whatever doesn't fit in the camper. *What a nice guy.* I grab some tissues for my bloody nose that keeps coming back and get back to moving.

I'm nearing the border of Canada. There's no traffic on this road whatsoever. Still haven't seen another thru-hiker in days.

Woof woof. Awooof.

I hear a dog barking in the distance. Two minutes later I see it, maybe a quarter mile away in a pasture barking at me. I keep walking in that direction. Soon another dog joins in on the barking.

I'm not fazed by them at first. I've passed many dogs barking at me on this trip. That's what dogs do—they bark. As I get closer to passing by, they come closer to the road. Now there are three dogs. One comes out onto the road in front of me, some kind of cattle dog mix. It's viciously barking and snarling, showing its teeth. I talk to it softly, trying to let it know I'm not a threat.

Then a German Shepherd mix comes around on the other side. It snaps and it snorts. *Are they flanking me?* I pick up a rock on the side of the road, just in case I need it. It's heavy enough to do some damage but light enough to move quickly. I keep talking to them in a calm voice. *They just need to know I'm not a threat.*

Ar, ar, ar, ar!

Soon I'm surrounded by three full-size dogs, all barking and snarling.

They've formed a triangle around me. I can see all three dogs' teeth. Drool drips out of one of their mouths.

Grrrrr.

The first dog stops barking, growls and holds its ground. It hunkers down, full mohawk from its neck to its tail, snarling at me in the nastiest way. As it snarls and it snorts, the other two keep barking ferociously.

My heart is pumping.

I keep talking to them like everything is fine and walk forward, slowly. I get closer and closer to the first dog. Eventually it backs up, keeping a short distance from me. A few minutes later, I'm able to get around it. All three stay behind. They continue barking at me from a distance until I'm out of sight.

Phew! That'll wake you up! They were just guarding their territory.

Before I realize it, I've gone another eight miles. As I'm looking at my map, I'm dumbfounded to see I've walked past an RV park, a store, and even the road that crosses into Canada—and I don't recall any of it. I've found this zombie-like trance of a power walk cruising at 3.5 miles per hour, not taking any wrong turns, but not remembering any of it either. *Where did those miles go?*

With only a few more miles of easy flats before the big climb over Abercrombie Mountain, I decide I'd better make the most of it. *Time to run.* I book it the next six miles to Cedar Lake and then take a break before making the 5,000-foot ascent. Looking at the map, the visual of all the switchbacks is intimidating. *It'll be good to have rested legs before I start.*

I wash my legs off in the lake; they're filthy. I can easily see all the cuts and scrapes on my shins and calves now, too many to count. My feet still have signs of trench foot. My shoes and socks are still soaking wet. I lay them out to dry, but the sun isn't out and everything outside is still damp; they don't stand a chance of drying. My feet look like they're rotting. The small black-pitted holes in the bottom of my feet are getting worse. *And here I was thinking my feet were getting better.* New shoes and socks in Metaline Falls tomorrow, though. AND I'm almost a week away from the finish line. *Just keep moving.*

On the way up Abercrombie Mountain, it's not raining, but all the overgrowth crowding out the trail is still dripping. As my legs brush up against the vegetation, water transfers to my legs and runs down to my shoes and socks. My feet aren't just wet anymore; they are submerged. They are swimming in the pool of water that's collecting in my shoes faster than it can dump out the sides.

This can't be good for my trench foot. *At least I'll have new shoes and socks tomorrow.*

The scenery changes again. Aspens. The colors of fall are emerging. It smells like Montana mountains. I must be getting close to Idaho.

The climb up Abercrombie is strangely easier than I expect. Seeing all the switchbacks on the map and knowing it's a 5,000-foot climb told me it would be a doozy, but the switchbacks are here to break it up. It's a slow, gentle ascent—a long one, but easy.

Once I make it to the top, I stop to change my socks. My other pair is still wet, but they are at least drier than the pair I'm wearing right now. I inspect my cold, wet, wrinkly, pitty feet. They look like rot. Leprosy mixed with a dying brain. I sit there, letting my feet air out, and think about what needs to be done. *I have to fix this foot problem ASAP. Please, please lend me some help. I can't let this get any worse.*

I originally planned to camp six miles outside of Metaline Falls tonight, then have a big breakfast and resupply in the morning—but if I book it, I might be able to make it to town before the grocery store closes. Maybe I can find something to help my feet there. *Maybe a blow dryer? That would certainly dry out my feet out.*

Texting Hannah, I ask her to look up remedies for trench foot and when the market closes; my cell service isn't strong enough for internet searches. Metaline Falls is a small town; the grocer is likely my best bet. She lets me know they close at 9:00 p.m. I check the map. I'm still 16 miles away. *If I run the whole way I can make it.*

I start running as fast as I can. *I have to get there before they close.* Hannah starts sending me remedies for trench foot, "Stay off your feet, don't wear shoes or socks, let them dry out, rest, wash them in hot soapy water." As I'm reading the solutions, I'm taken aback. *I can't do any of these without slowing down.* Then she says, "Foot powder." *Ah, yes, I can do that. The grocery store surely has some foot powder.*

I make it to Metaline Falls quicker than I anticipate. Apparently I can run faster than I thought. I walk in the shop just before 8:00 p.m., and the clerk remarks, "You made it just in time. I was about to close up."

"I thought you guys closed at 9:00 p.m.?"

"Those are our summer hours. It's basically fall here now. We just changed to 8:00."

"Sorry! I'll make it quick. Where's your foot powder?"

"We don't have any foot powder. Your best bet would be the pharmacy across the street when they open up tomorrow at 10:00 a.m."

"10:00 a.m.? I can't wait that long. I'm kind of in a hurry."

A guy, probably in his late 20s, overhears the conversations and speaks up, "Hey, I have some medicated Gold Bond in my car. I got it for basketball, but I honestly can't stand it. It's too messy. You can have it if you want."

"THANK YOU!!! You're a godsend."

The bottle of foot powder he gives me is massive—the size of a football. *I'll take it.* Normally I'm concerned about size and weight because I have to carry everything on my back. But I don't care in this situation; I'll take anything I can get. "Thank you, thank you, thank you. You have no idea how bad I need this. Want to see my feet?"

"No," he laughs. "I don't need to see your feet. I'm just glad it's out of my car."

"Thank you again. I really appreciate it."

I grab my resupply box, some pizza at the town bar, and head to set up camp in a local trail angel's yard. It's the most civilized place I've slept on the entire trip. It's right on the edge of downtown Metaline Falls, all two city blocks of it. If I peek around the corner of their building, I can see the movie theater, grocery store, breakfast diner, evening bar, post office, and a quilt shop. That's pretty much most of downtown Metaline Falls. DeForest, one of the trail angels that lives here, hands me an extension cord and shows me their hiker box. *I get to charge my batteries overnight!?* My mind is blown. I'm so thankful.

After laying out my quilt, I organize my resupplies and begin to doctor my feet. I start with a heaping amount of Gold Bond, making sure to coat every bit of skin with the white messy residue. In between each toe, over the heels, rubbing my arches. It's turning it into a powdery foot massage. Once they are completely covered, I dump even more on them before lying down with my feet on either side of my bivy—trying to relax while not caking flour all over my gear.

New, dry shoes and socks. Foot powder. Full power to charge batteries overnight. A flat, soft, cushy yard to sleep in. And pizza. It's a good ending to a 50.8-mile day.

But I'm clueless as to what I'll be going through tomorrow.

IDAHO'S WARM WELCOME

TODAY'S GOAL: make it to mile 939.9 trail camp. This will get me a few miles into Idaho, not too far from the Lion's Creek Bushwhack Scramble. The hardest bushwhack of the PNT.

As I'm walking up the highway coming out of Metaline Falls, my lower stomach begins to feel uneasy. And not in a pukey way, in a poopy way. *Was it the pizza last night?* Moments later, I realize I'm not even going to make it away from the highway. Diarrhea calls. And there's nothing I can do. It's barely after 4:00 a.m. *Thank goodness there's no one out here.* I pop a squat on the side of the highway, just off the shoulder. It's one of those moments where you have to dig the cat hole afterward. *Sorry folks.*

I keep moving and keep stopping for squirting. *They're after me this morning.* Third time today, and the sun's not even up.

The sunrise over Sullivan Creek makes me smile. Pinks, purples, and blues. The sky is covered in colorful clouds. The trees are lush, and the creek is rushing. *I'm definitely not in a desert anymore.*

I come across a trash can shortly before the first big climb of the day. What can I throw away? What can I get rid of to lose some weight? I just resupplied in Metaline Falls, so my pack is back to heavy. I eat a few dense items that produce trash, so I don't have to deal with the extra garbage for the next few days. I'm a week from finishing at this pace. I clip my toenails one last time and throw away the clippers. I throw some more foot powder on my feet and douse the insides of my shoes while I'm at it. I'll have more Aquaphor at my next resupply in three days—I throw away my extra. Won't need this athletic tape either; it goes too.

By noon, I'm on top of a mountain ridge on my way toward Upper Priest Lake. It's proving to be an overcast day. I'm thankful the sun is blocked out to allow for cooler temperatures, but it hasn't had a chance to dry any of the vegetation. As I walk through the overgrowth, water from the plants runs down my legs and into my shoes again. My brand-new dry shoes are already wet. I still have a dry pair of socks from my resupply box in Metaline Falls, but there's no point in putting them on because they would just get wet too.

I wonder what my feet look like. Are they all wrinkled and pitted? Do they still look like they're rotting? Or are they covered in a thick paste of wet foot powder since I so generously coated the insides of my shoes earlier?

I reach an open area with no trees or overgrown plants. I touch the grass next to the trail. It's dry. I take my shoes off to wring out my socks. Dark, dirty water drips out. *Hmm. No powder paste.* Where did all the powder go? I slip my socks back on—they're still wet, but they have to be better than they were now that they've been wrung out, right? I dump more Gold Bond in my shoes.

Five minutes later, I'm back to thick, wet vegetation crowding out the trail. My socks are back to soaked. That stop was pointless.

I meet a hunter on the way up the next mountain. He's carrying a beige bag with a bear head in it. He shows me the head. *Yup. That's a black bear.* His hunting buddy is just a short ways behind him with the rest of the meat. *Does bear meat even taste good?*

He cautions, "Lots of bears are up in this area. Do you have a pistol?"

"No."

"Do you have bear spray?"

"No."

"Do you have any type of protection!?"

"I'm picking up an air horn in Idaho."

He stares at me with his jaw dropped.

"Bear spray is too heavy and bulky."

"Where are you headed?"

"Montana."

"Are you on that Pacific Northwest Trail?"

"Yeah."

"So you started at the Pacific Ocean? Isn't that like 800 miles away from here? When did you start?"

"Yeah, yeah, on August 23rd."

"You left the Pacific Ocean at the end of August. Like, just a couple of weeks ago, August?"

"Yeah." I'm getting drilled with questions.

"No way. Most people I run into have been on the trail for at least a month. And they're going the opposite direction. They're just getting started."

"Well, I'm kind of doing it fast."

"There's a decent campsite like five more miles ahead you can stop at. That's where we were last night."

"Oh, thanks, but I still have a ways to go tonight. I'm trying to get to Upper Priest Lake."

"That's like another 25 miles away! You're crazy." He turns around and shouts to his hunting buddy down the trail, "This guy left the Olympic Peninsula on August 23rd, and he's doing a million miles a day—on foot! He's headed to Upper Priest Lake tonight."

A few miles later the sun comes out. I'm on top of a mountain ridge. I still haven't seen another thru-hiker in days. I just saw those two hunters, but I didn't see any other cars at the trailhead. *I've got the trail to myself again.* My shorts are wet with sweat. Off they go. I'll air-dry them as I walk.

I wave my shorts through the air as I trudge along, attempting to give them more air flow so they can dry faster. *Yup. That's me. Naked guy walking on top of a mountain ridge, waving his shorts through the air like a flag.* My arms don't have the endurance that my legs do, though. Within minutes my shorts are hanging off my backpack.

I'm either staring off into the distant views daydreaming, or absolutely not paying attention, because when I look up the trail I see two more hunters only 50 feet away, walking straight toward me. I stop dead in my tracks. I'm on an exposed ridge. There are no trees, no bushes, no boulders—nothing to hide behind—just me and my naked self. I drop to the ground, put my shorts back on, stand up, and keep walking toward them.

"Sorry about that," I whisper as I walk by.

They're silent. Not a sound. Brief eye contact, but they keep on their way as we pass within inches of each other. *Quiet because they are hunting, or quiet because they are disturbed by my nakedness?*

Hours later, on the way down the mountain, nearing the border of Idaho, I'm caught in a torrential downpour. Soon the trail is a couple of inches deep in rainwater. Blowdowns are slippery and exhausting to get over. The winds are high. The rain is heavy. I hear trees collapsing in the forest. Lightning flashes all around.

I keep slipping and falling in the mud. My legs are weak, but I need them to be strong.

The turns aren't marked for the PNT. I'm struggling to keep my GPS screen operational in the rain. It's getting dark, and it's getting cold. When I finally reach the trailhead, I'm back on forest service roads until I get back on another foot trail.

I come to a fork in the road, but there aren't any signs. I don't know where I'm at. I have no clue which way to go, and I can't get my GPS to operate to tell me which turn to take. *But it feels like Upper Priest Lake is to the right.* I go right.

I'm stressed, tired, cold, and wet. Something's got to give. I'm praying for a miracle.

All of a sudden I come across a bridge with a flat spot underneath it. It's Fort Dry Bridge. I take shelter, figure out where I'm at, and take advantage of the smooth, level area just big enough for one person under it.

After laying out my bivy, quilt, sleeping pad, and some snacks for the night, I go through my nightly stretches, foot massage, and "doctor the chafing spots" routine while I think about what has to happen tomorrow. I'm nine miles behind schedule, but at least I've crossed into Idaho. *Barely.* Tomorrow is the Lion's Creek Bushwhack, the hardest bushwhack of the PNT. It's six miles long, and I'm still 28 miles from the *beginning* of it. I HAVE to get through it while the sun is up and it HAS to be good weather; otherwise, it could be a nightmare.

How long will it take to get through? I read all the comments I can find about it on Guthooks. It took several people eight hours. One person claims they did it in seven. *But it only took Encore four.* They were all going downhill. I'll be going uphill. I decide to allot myself five to six hours. *If I give myself a decent amount of time and just take it nice and easy, I won't be as mentally defeated like I was on the last bad bushwhack.* Daylight hours are getting shorter and shorter. I'd better start moving at 2:00 a.m.

THE BUSHWHACK

IT'S 1:45 A.M. I don't hear rain anymore. I peek out from under the bridge I slept under and can see the stars—the rain clouds are gone. Today is going to be a good day. Time to get moving.

I have to make it past the hardest bushwhack of the PNT today. I'm thankful it's not raining. *Just stay this way for 34 miles.* Rain would make traveling through the bushwhack ten times harder. Debris would be slicker. It'd be harder to navigate. My GPS would be difficult to operate. Maps would be hard to use. The longer I'm in there, the higher likelihood the sun will go down. And if I'm still in there when it gets dark, it could get nasty. Not to mention traveling through crazy-thick brush in the middle of the dark is just simply a bad idea in grizzly country. I am in Idaho now, after all.

Not only do I hope it doesn't rain, I hope the sun comes out. I need it to dry out my gear. Nearly everything I have is wet. The only dry pieces of kit I have at this point are my quilt, sleeping pad, bivy, and puffy jacket. *At least my sleep setup isn't wet.*

By 4:30 a.m., I'm on foot trails skirting the edge of Upper Priest Lake. The ground and plants are still sopping. The trail is a long, on-going puddle of water. Remnants from yesterday's storm percolate through the trees onto my head and shoulders. Rain isn't falling from the sky, but my feet are staying wet nevertheless.

It would be fun to explore if I had more time and if everything wasn't so wet. The forest is lush and green, full of oxygen. Thick ferns cover the ground, and giant cedars tower the trails. Their canopies block out the stars—at least I hope. *Are the trees blocking out the stars, or are clouds rolling in? Please don't rain. Just hold off until I get through the bushwhack.*

A light hue begins to cover the earth. The sun will be up soon. The trees part, and I get a good view overlooking the lake. It's transcendent.

Clouds cover the majority of the sky, but a few gaps allow the final stars of the night to shine through. A fog rolls over the far side of the lake, falling from the trees above and sliding across the water. The soft colors of the early sunrise are inviting. *It IS going to be a good day.*

I start feeling a lot of friction between my pinky toes. *Not today, blisters.* I stop to inspect. I haven't had a single blister out here so far—which I credit to proactively taking care of my feet as much as possible, and my shoes. Despite how bad my arches have been hurting, I love my shoes.

Still no blisters—but with how soft, wet, and wrinkly my feet are, it's only a matter of time before one pops up today if I don't make a change. I douse some foot powder and scrunch on my toe socks; they're still wet, but they have to be better than nothing between my toes.

Hours later, I make it to the start of the bushwhack sooner than I anticipate. I don't want to take a break, but I know once I'm in it, I'm not likely to get a clear open spot to do so. I stop and climb up to sit on a large concrete block that's stopping vehicles from continuing into the forest—it's the end of the dirt road. The block is covered in blue and purple graffiti. Despite the vandalism, I welcome it as art. It's somehow comforting and fresh.

The sun still isn't out. The clouds have grown thicker. I'm beginning to lose hope that I'll get a chance to dry anything out today. *Please, just don't rain. At least don't rain until I get through the bushwhack. Just let me get through the bushwhack.*

Despite there being no sun, I take my shoes and socks off to inspect and give my feet some air time. They are still disgustingly pitty. The dark, black, rotty mess is growing and spreading across the bottom of my feet. I wipe my feet with my socks; the black won't come off. I scrub, still nothing. I generously sprinkle foot powder on them, inside my socks and inside my shoes—still surprised I'm not creating a white paste with how wet everything is.

I look down at my legs. They look thin, scraggly. My ankles appear to have tan lines, but I know they're just filthy. Countless cuts and scrapes are scattered across my shins. *These things have carried me 950 miles. Only 300 more to go.*

At 9:30 a.m., I start working my way through the bushwhack. *Oh, this isn't so bad.* A decent social trail is forming from all the other hikers that have gone through this year. Every once in a while I lose the trail, but I seem to stumble back across it fairly quickly.

I hear a low-pitched growl. It quickly progresses to a high-pitched scream. *Elk.* It's close.

Searching to find it, I navigate around a clump of trees. And there she is, a full-grown cow, standing in an open meadow. She tilts her head back and screams again. I raise my phone to get a video; my arm bumps a bush in the process. She looks at me and then darts off into the forest. *How did my arm brushing against this little bush scare her off, but when I walked around the corner to get over here, it didn't even faze her?*

By the time I've been in the bushwhack for an hour, I've already traveled over two miles. *Pshhhh. This is nothing. I don't get why all the comments on Guthooks indicated it would take such a long time to get through here.* It's nothing compared to the bushwhack scramble up Edd's Mountain, where I only made it a half-mile in the course of an hour.

The social trail slowly turns into a game trail. Maybe it was just a game trail all along? Eventually it fades. I've lost it, and this time I can't find it. *I jinxed myself.*

The bushes grow thicker. Taller than I am. Every time I touch a shrub, it shakes, raining water left over from last night down on me. It feels like I'm picking up another pound in water weight for every 10 feet of travel. The blowdowns are so big; I have to take the rain kilt off to be able to lift my legs high enough to get over them.

I keep one of my hands lifted high in the air, to not touch any of the wet vegetation, to keep my fingers dry. I use that hand to operate my GPS screen. *How did I lose the path?*

I keep moving forward, sometimes holding onto bushes to help climb up the steep slope—sometimes parting the bushes to give myself a way to get through. All this, with one arm straight up in the air. *I look like a Nazi.*

As I drag my feet through the complex tangle of bushes, limbs, and twigs, a branch slaps the bottom of my left shin. *Ahhhh!* It stings. *That's going to leave a bruise.* It's not the first branch to slap my shin through this mess, but it's definitely the worst.

I keep climbing my way through the jungle as it keeps tripping me up. The tendon between my shin and the top of my left foot is nearly unbearable. The pain is shattering. This certainly isn't the first day it's bugged me, but the pain and tightness have elevated to an entirely new level. *Was it the twig slap? All the tripping over bushes?*

I try moving down in elevation, hoping to escape the wreckage. It turns into a marsh. The wet ground sinks under my feet. *OK, I'll try the other side.* I start scrambling up, and it just gets worse. I check the map. *This is not the direction I need to be traveling. Guess I'll just keep going through the brush.*

Every time I trip over something with my left foot, forcing that foot to bend down and backward, that tendon screams. I can barely lift my foot by the ankle anymore because it's so tight.

Just keep moving.

My feet crunch on ice chunks, marble-sized hail. *It must have hailed up here last night in that storm.* I keep climbing; the piles of ice get bigger and bigger. I find a pile large enough to lay my shin and foot on. I lean forward and lay the top of my foot, ankle, and shin on the ice—nearly kneeling. It's soothing.

As I approach the top of the pass, still fighting my way through the thick, I see a downed tree with a boulder next to it. The tree is at an uphill angle. It could be slick, but to me—it's a bridge of opportunity. *If I could get on that tree, I could climb up and pass 25 feet of this terrain much easier. I wouldn't have to fight all this brush.* I scramble up the tree, holding onto various broken-off limbs to maintain control. I'm thankful for the bridge. It gives me a break, a chance to move forward while avoiding the tangled mess of plants below.

Eventually I make it out of the nasty part of the bushwhack, to the top of the ridge where the ground is mostly covered in granite slabs and boulders. The dense growth has dissipated. I'm still not on an actual trail yet, but moving has become easy again.

Up at 6,700 feet, the trees thin out and the views open. The clouds are thick and low, covering the peaks and a majority of the scenery—but it's alluring. I shuffle through the fog along the ridgeline, hurdling down boulders and up ledges. Gnarled pines and firs poke through the clouds with their shadows. It's earthy, wet, and alive. The smell is intoxicating. It's mystical. Seductive. Powerful. It's one of those places where the mountains just want to hold on to you.

It's 2:00 p.m. I've already been on my feet for 12 hours, but the hardest part of the PNT is now behind me. Some of it was easier than I expected, some of it worse. I perk up. Confidence surges. I'm eager for the next piece of the puzzle. *Hardest part of the PNT is out of the way; FKT, here I come!*

I stop to let my feet air out again. They've been soaking wet all day long; I'm dreading what they look like. I peel off my socks to inspect. From when I looked at them before the bushwhack till now, they looked like they've progressed three more days of complete submersion underwater. Wrinkly white, splotchy with light shades of pink, and littered with black polka dots of disgusting, rotty-mold-looking nastiness. A little tingly. A little itchy. It feels good to scratch them—but if I scratch too hard, chunks scrape off under my fingernails. *Is that good or is that bad?* I dust powder on them and lean back on a log.

A few minutes go by. *I shouldn't stop here. I need to stop when there's full sun out so I can dry gear at the same time.* I slip my wet socks on and stand back up in my shoes. *I'll stop as soon as the sun comes out.*

Why do I keep having these steep climbs? In my head I had pictured being done with climbs after I finished the bushwhack. After the scramble, I'd be up on a ridge. I'd be up on top of the mountain; it's all downhill after that, right?

Wrong.

The ridgeline goes up and down, and up and down, and up and down.

Just a few days ago Encore was texting me, telling me that my steepest climbs were still ahead, "Idaho and Montana are no joke." He wasn't kidding. *These climbs are way steeper than the climbs in Washington.* Either that, or I'm just really tired.

A few hours later, my bottles are nearly empty, so I check the water sources on my map. I'm dumbfounded. As it turns out, I'm on a dry 18-mile ridgeline. I've been so excited to be out of the bushwhack I haven't been paying attention. *Should have filled up at Pyramid Lake.*

And again, I'm left with a carrot to pull me a few miles farther. I originally planned to camp at elevation somewhere, but the next stream is all the way at the base of the range. *Guess I'm getting off the mountain tonight.*

At the top of Long Mountain, the sun finally decides to come out through a break in the clouds. *This is my chance.* I lay out all my gear on warm, dry granite boulders that clearly have been getting plenty of sun. I kick off my shoes and set an alarm. *Just a ten-minute snooze while everything dries.*

My alarm goes off. I open my eyes and look straight up at the sky. The clouds are back.

I check my gear; my tarp and bivy are dry, but everything else is still wet. I pack it all up and quickly get on my way.

About five miles later, I come across a small puddle on a granite boulder. It's a rain puddle from last night. It's too shallow to dip my bottle in so I lean over it. Lip to puddle, I suck the water up. It's quenching and crisp. Life giving. I drink a few more long sips and get back on my feet.

By the time I've been on my feet for 19 hours, I'm completely spent. It's already been dark for a couple of hours and the night is dragging. My eyes keep closing as I stumble forward. I have to slap myself in the face just to stay awake. My legs are ready to stop, but I know I can't yet. I have to get to water. *Just keep moving.*

Just 3 more miles.

Just 2 more miles.

Just 1 more mile.

Eventually, I make it to the trailhead at the base of the Selkirk Mountains. I refill my bottles in a stream under a bridge and lie down in the only flat spot between the trail and the road. *You're sleeping five feet from a road? That's real smart, Nick. Real smart.* But I don't care. I'm too tired to care. *It's a low-traffic road. It'll be fine.*

It's just before 10:00 p.m.: 45.7 miles in 20 hours. *Barf.* That took way too long, but the big bushwhack is now behind me. Tomorrow will be better. Tomorrow I'll get to Feist Creek Resort, where I'll pick up my resupply and grizzly bear protection: my airhorn.

CHEERIOS AND CHOCOLATE BARS

I WAKE UP TO WETNESS. My quilt is damp. My bivy and shoes have been PNT'd—they're drenched.

I instantly know where I messed up. Last night, I camped without setting my tarp. The stars were out; there wasn't a single cloud in the sky. I figured if it started raining it would wake me up, and I could just get under my tarp quickly. It doesn't take much to pitch it in a pinch.

But what I wasn't thinking about was dew. Condensation. The silent soaker.

And now everything is soaked. *What a rookie mistake.* Camping on grass is asking for it. Grass always gets dew in the morning, especially when it's near water. I was so tired last night I just wanted to lie down and go to sleep as soon as possible. I wasn't thinking about the consequences.

Alright. This is the homestretch. Five days left after today. *Let's do this!* By noon I should be picking up my resupply at Feist Creek, and by tonight I'll be in Montana.

I rolled and massaged my shin last night. I think it helped, but it's still incredibly tense and painful.

A thick fog settles over the flat, open pastures around the Kootenai River. A family of eight deer prance alongside the bank. Some trotting, some walking. Half move in unison, graceful like synchronized dancers. The sun hasn't finished coming up; it's mainly their silhouettes that I watch near the end of my visibility in the fog. It's the perfect scene. The magic never ceases out here.

I pass the 1,000-mile mark for eastbounders. It's not that remarkable. It's on a forest service road in a mediocre forest—mediocre compared to the Olympics or North Cascades. Every time I've seen a thru-hiker surpass this milestone on social media, regardless of the trail, they have rocks laid out, spelling out the 1,000. But I don't have that. All I have is a dirt road. I feel robbed. Even so, the fact that I've crossed a thousand continuous miles by foot, for the first time in my life, pumps excitement through my veins. *Only 250 to go!*

I come across another mine shaft. Sixty-second detour! *Who am I kidding? It's never just 60 seconds.* I run up to it; it's barred up and closed off to access. *Lame.* I snap a photo and get back on trail. *Ha, I guess it actually was just 60 seconds this time.* Funny, I don't have a problem detouring for a mine, but I refuse to take the time to write out 1,000 in rocks. *Priorities.*

Up and over Bussard Mountain. I feel like I'm making good time on the way down the other side. I pass by a trail crew taking a break. We chat for a couple of minutes, and I continue on my way. All of a sudden, I hit a dead end. *Crap.* I check the map.

Dang it!

Somehow I missed a turn and went 1.3 miles in the wrong direction. *How did I miss that turn?*

1.3 miles DOWNHILL in the wrong direction. I'm beating myself up as I hike back up the mountain. *There goes thirty minutes. Times two. You just lost an hour, Nick.*

As I'm headed back uphill, I pass the trail crew again. "Why didn't you tell me I was headed in the wrong direction?"

"Are you on the Pacific Northwest Trail?"

"Yeah."

"Sorry. We didn't know where you were headed. People are constantly stealing the PNT markers out here. We replace them from time to time, but they always end up missing."

Why are people such douchebags?

When I make it back to the junction where I was supposed to turn, I see why I missed it. I continued straight on the forest service road when I should have turned off on a faint trail to the right. The only indicator marking the turn is a small, three-rock cairn, likely stacked by some hikers at some point.

I make it to Feist Creek Resort. It's a blessing to the PNT because they'll hold resupply boxes for you. There's no other form of grocery, convenience, or even general store out here—no other options for a resupply. It's just this small hotel and a restaurant that's open on the weekends. And today is Wednesday.

I walk through the property, past the restaurant and toward the hotel rooms. I'm looking for the office. An employee sees me and asks, "Are you a thru-hiker?"

"Yes. I sent a resupply box here."

"Here, come with me."

He unlocks the restaurant, and we walk inside. He leads me to their stairs toward the back and points to a stack of resupply boxes. But my box isn't there.

Effffff.

All the goods to get me to Eureka—my food, ibuprofen, even my air horn for some form of bear protection in grizzly country—all not here. There's no cell service, but thankfully the restaurant has wifi. I ask for the password and message Hannah to check the tracking.

What am I going to do?

Justin, the employee who's been helping me, offers to open up their grill and cook me a meal.

"Oh, thank you so much. You really have no idea what this means to me."

I hear back from Hannah about the tracking. My box is "still in transit." Who knows when it'll get here. It could be later this afternoon, tomorrow, or even next week. I can't wait for that. *At least I can eat a hot meal while I sit here and figure out what to do.*

Justin makes me a burger, a massive mound of french fries, and serves me an ice-cold can of Dr Pepper. Moments of rest are strange out here. Despite the missing box I feel a sense of ease. I'm not looking at the clock. I have an excuse to not rush while I eat. A few Dr Peppers later, they are down to just one can left. I restrain myself.

I start going through their hiker box for unwanted food left behind by other hikers. I find a jar of sunflower seed spread and a couple of meals I can cold soak: some dehydrated chili and a Mountain House chicken fried rice meal.

Soon another employee comes into the restaurant. Julie has a strong English accent. Her personality is hilarious. She tells me stories of the owner of the resort flying her all over the state to help her get her immigration paperwork taken care of. Then she suddenly changes topics and asks me, "Do you bodybuild?"

"No... why?"

"Because you've got the biggest legs that have been through here all year."

We both start laughing.

The owner, Cliff, walks in. Justin and Julie start explaining my situation to him. He offers, "We have some cereal and fruit you can have. Does that help?" "Yes! I'll take anything I can get at this point. Thank you." We chat for a bit. He says he used to have a pet black bear and mountain lion. I don't believe him at first. Then he takes me to a wall in the restaurant and shows me pictures of him and his wife holding the lion. A full-size cougar, in their lap, on their couch. "But the bear was much easier to train," he explains. "Bears are trainable like dogs. Mountain lions are cats, and cats are—well—they are cats. Cats like to do their own thing."

Cliff disappears and returns a little while later with a box of Cheerios, along with some strawberries and cranberries left over from a wedding they catered the weekend before.

I lay out the food I raided from the hiker box with the new addition of Cheerios and fruit. *That's still not enough food to get me to Eureka.* I've been eating so much. I need more fuel. I look up at the wall behind their register. They have chocolate bars for sale.

"OK, I'm going to order a big basket of fries to go... and I'll take all your Paydays, all your Milky Ways, all your M&Ms, all your Whatchamacallits, all the Kit Kats, the Rolos, and all the Carmellos." *Why don't they have Snickers?*

Everyone but me starts busting up laughing.

"No, I'm serious."

Now we're all laughing together.

"And I'll take your last Dr Pepper to go."

After three hours of mingling, eating, charging up devices, and letting my gear air out on the deck outside, I get moving—with $50 worth of chocolate bars. That stop took way too long, but hey, my box didn't show up, and I'm actually leaving with food. That turned out OK.

All my gear is dry. Most importantly, my shoes and socks. I just need to keep it this way. *I HAVE to keep my feet dry.* I'm not sure how much more wet they can handle.

Dark clouds roll in after I leave Feist Creek. I cross my fingers, hoping it doesn't rain. *Or at least just hold off until I get to Montana. Then you can start raining.*

What starts as a sprinkle, slowly grows heavier. I check the map; I'm only a handful of miles from Montana now. *If I can just make it across the border.* I start running uphill as fast as I can, holding on to the hope that I might be able to get to the state line before I get completely drenched. *Just keep your feet dry. Just keep your feet dry.*

The rain picks up even more. I begin to question if I should stop sooner, just set up camp in the next flat spot before my shoes get soaked. Then, the rain lightens back up. *OK, maybe I actually can make it to Montana before it starts dumping.*

I'm only a mile away from the border. The sun's down. The rain has grown heavier than I told myself I'd continue hiking in to make sure my feet stay dry, but here I am still hiking. I haven't seen a level clearing wide enough for camp.

Just as I make it to Montana, right on the border, I find a flat spot wide enough. *Bingo.* It begins to pour. *Just in time.* I pitch my tarp faster than I've ever done before, throw my gear underneath, and dive in.

As I'm massaging my feet I notice a spider. It looks like a granddaddy long leg, but not. It's crawling over the foot end of my bivy. I flick it off. I keep massaging my feet and look to the left. Another eight-legged creature is crawling over my groundsheet. I flick that one away too.

I turn my headlamp on brighter and look all around. Dozens of web-spinners are creeping under my tarp, all seemingly headed straight toward me. *They must be trying to escape the rain too. Or maybe they're attracted to my headlamp?* I flick five more away. *I can't do this all night.* I tuck away inside my bivy and zip it up, completely enclosing myself.

I think about the last couple of days. Torrential-downpour thunderstorm and sleeping under a bridge near the border of Washington and Idaho. The Lion's Creek Bushwhack. My box not showing up at Feist Creek. Now I'm at the border of Idaho and Montana with a bunch of spiders. *Two days to get through Idaho. Even with all those obstacles.* What an adventure.

I'm so tired; the spiders don't even bother me as I fall asleep.

---- DAY 24 ----

MONTANA

I WAKE UP AT 3:00 A.M. There's a Whatchamacallit in my mouth. I was so tired last night that I fell asleep before I finished chewing it.

Efficiency. Breakfast is served.

I'm moving by 3:30, which is actually 4:30 since I'm in Montana now. My phone and watch just haven't caught up with the time zone switch yet. Thankfully, it's not raining anymore. The stars are out in full array; there's not a cloud in sight.

My shoes and socks are damp from the rain last night, but not drenched. However, the trails are overgrown, and all the vegetation is wet. Which means my shoes, socks, and feet are soon to be drowning in water again.

Owoooooooooooo.

I hear wolves howling in the distance. They say you can hear a wolf's howl up to six miles away in the woods. *If you take the median, does that mean they are more like three miles away?* I've seen these beasts in Yellowstone before, but that was right next to a road. This is truly in the wilderness. *It would be so cool if I get to see a wolf out here!*

I look up at the sky. Stars are everywhere; so many, they light up the trail. It's the thickest I've seen the Milky Way since starting the PNT. I still haven't seen a thru-hiker since the Pasayten Wilderness either. I have the whole mountain to myself. *How special is this?* I'm sore, tired, hungry, and depleted. I'm moving so slow. But I have this whole mountain to myself, and it's bliss. Just me, the mountains, the trees, and the stars.

And the wolves. Let's not forget about the wolves.

Signs are posted on trees sporadically out here: "THIS IS GRIZZLY BEAR COUNTRY. Hunters: Know your bears. Campers: Keep a clean camp. Hikers: Be alert on trails."

OK, and the grizzly bears. Just me, the mountains, the wolves, and the grizzly bears.

By late morning, I'm feeling feeble and frail. Living on Cheerios and chocolate bars isn't giving me the energy that I've grown to expect from all the nuts, carbs, and protein-rich foods I've been living on for the last thousand miles.

I'm dizzy. Light headed. My body and arms are tingling. *Ugh… I don't have my electrolytes since my resupply box didn't show up. And my food options don't have much salt either.*

I hear a bear chuffing. I look to the left, but I don't see it. I hear it again and look up. It's a grizzly cub in a tree about 50 feet away. First bear I've ever seen in a tree! We make eye contact and pause—then it climbs up farther into the canopy and disappears. *Wow, they're fast climbers.*

OK, but where's mom?

I love grizzlies. They're cuter and fluffier than their black bear cousins. They have the rounded ears and plump face of a teddy. And they're chunkier—better for cuddles. But they're grumpy and have mood swings. I wouldn't want to get too close to mom.

My left shin is swollen; I assume from that tendon that's so tight and inflamed. It hurts to run, hurts to walk. But it's less painful to walk.

Only five days left. Keep moving.

I just want to be done. Hannah is my light at the end of the tunnel. I just want to lie down next to her and be done.

Maybe I just need solid, real food energy. I start eating the sunflower seed spread straight from the jar with a plastic spoon.

The sun comes out, but it won't be for long. The clouds are on the move. I'll stop and take what I can get. I lay out my socks and inspect my feet. They don't look good, but they look better than they did yesterday. Maybe the foot powder and routine stops to air out my feet are helping.

I close my eyes with another ten-minute alarm, but I can't fall asleep for some reason. I end up just eating a couple of chocolate bars until the sun disappears behind more clouds.

Keep moving.

I'm on the verge of mentally breaking. Tears have been on edge several times today. I'm tired. I'm just so tired.

Bang!

Gunshot. Super close by. *Hunters.* I don't have anything that's orange anymore. My original microfiber towel was my orange item, but of course I lost that on week one.

I walk around the corner and see a hunter loading his dog into the back of a red Dodge pickup.

"Did you get one?"

"Oh yeah. There were three. Got one, but it fell down in the ravine. I've gotta go dig it out. Are you hiking that Pacific North Something Trail?"

"Yes, sir, I am."

"Hang on a sec." He reaches into the back of his truck and pulls out a Coors Banquet. "Here. Crack this open when you get to the top of Mount Henry."

CALORIES! "Thank you!"

Once I'm back on foot trails, the overcast skies gradually darken. *I hope it doesn't rain again.*

An elk runs across the trail, not too far in front of me. It's graceful in how well it carries its weight. Five hundred pounds of meat swiftly gliding through the forest. If it weren't for its hooves, it'd be silent.

I make it to my goal destination for the night, 45 miles in. But I check the comments on Guthooks, and it turns out there are rats here:

"Rats still here. RIP sleep."

"Three pack rats attacked in the night."

"Don't be fooled by the nice campsite here. Rodents are extremely active."

There's no way I'll get any sleep with rats. I check the map. A lookout tower is on top of Mount Henry, about five miles away. *That would get some good sleep.*

The climb up Henry is steep and unrelenting. It just keeps going and going. It never stops. The sun is now completely gone. It's dark, cold, and windy. The only reason I'm not freezing is because I'm hauling butt trying to get up this mountain. I'm climbing so fast my body is an oven; it's as if I can actually feel my internal temperature increasing the faster I move. The sweat drips, but if I stop for just a few seconds it reverses, and the cold air hits—and it hits deep. *That's because you don't have any pants on, Nick.*

Eventually, I make it to the top of the trail, where it turns to start going back down the mountain. This is where the map indicated the lookout would be. But it's not. The sign in front of my face tells me the tower is another 0.2 miles uphill, out of the way.

It's the longest 0.2 miles of my life.

I'm bone-tired and frustrated. But when I see the tower at the summit, I'm hit with a wave of relief. *Finally.*

Suddenly, the door swings open, and someone yells, "We've got it nice and toasty in here for you."

People! Crap! I turn off my headlamp and complete the short-slip shuffle again. *Thank goodness it's pitch black out.*

I walk up the tower steps to be greeted by a couple of guys in their 20s, Jordan and Kenyon. "That's ballsy coming up here in the dark like this."

Shoot! Did they see?

They are super friendly. I'm super cranky.

I'm cold, depleted, and ready to go down. I was about to come in here and immediately crash, but these people are up here raiding my tower. Their friendliness quickly wins over my frustration, though—it's either that, the warm, cozy cabin, or simply the fact that I'm no longer climbing this mountain.

They have a fire going in the wood stove, and they're drinking Crown Royal. They offer me some. *Are you kidding me? That's calories.* It warms me from the inside, an inner sweater. They even offer me a burrito for breakfast. I turn hopeful, "Ummm. Can I have it now?" Jordan places it on top of the wood stove to warm it up for me. I explain I've hiked nearly 51 miles today, I'm on the PNT trying to set a new FKT, and my resupply box didn't show up yesterday. "So I'm living on Cheerios and chocolate bars. Well… the Cheerios are already gone."

Kenyon turns to Jordan, "I told you we would meet someone cool up here!"

Jordan gives me some ibuprofen; what a blessing. I'm out. I had some in my resupply box for Feist Creek to restock with, but we know how that turned out.

My mouth salivates as my teeth sink into the burrito. It's the best breakfast roll-up I've ever had, hands down. Eggs, sausage, cheese, and the carbs of a tortilla. I may be a little hunger-biased and in the moment. But this burrito… let me tell you. This burrito is what dreams are made of.

"Hey, I hope it's OK, but I'm going to try and go to sleep soon. I need to be moving by 4:00 a.m." They have zero-degree sleeping bags and full-size sleeping pads on the two wooden bed frames. I pull out my 40-degree quilt and x-frame sleeping pad that only takes two breaths to air up. I make my bed on the floor next to the wood stove.

I go through my nightly routine, getting ready for sleep and preparing for the morning. "You think if I put this on top of the stove in the morning, it'll be good?" I lift up my Mountain House meal from the hiker box at Feist Creek Resort. I've been procrastinating eating it, not wanting to deal with the hassle of cold soaking.

Jordan says, "You can use my stove in the morning." He brings it over and sets it on the table next to me. *You mean I'm going to have a warm meal for breakfast?*

Lying next to the wood stove, thoughts about the trail flood my mind. All the experiences and emotions I've gone through in such a short amount of time. And now I'm here—in a warm cabin, burrito in my belly, ibuprofen and Crown Royal in my blood, and a warm meal waiting for me in the morning.

It's a good ending to a tough day. I'm grateful.

SHOULDN'T HAVE DONE THAT

BRRRRR.

The cold wakes me. I'm shivering inside my quilt. This lookout tower on top of Mount Henry, just south of the Canadian border, is at 7,243 feet. I grab my phone for lighting to put my puffy coat and rain jacket on. It's 1:32 a.m. I got here just a few hours ago, but the fire in the wood stove has already gone out. I slip my quilt inside my bivy for a few extra degrees of warmth and try to get another two hours of sleep. My alarm is set to go off at 4:00 a.m.

After an hour of restless, cold, sleep attempts, I check the weather on my phone. It's 27 degrees at the base of the mountain, around 2,500 feet. That means it could be in the single digits up here. You lose three to five degrees in temperature for every 1,000 feet of elevation gain. The only clothes I have are a pair of two-inch running shorts, one sleeveless shirt, one long-sleeve shirt, a rain jacket, puffy coat, and two pairs of socks.

I restart the fire in the wood stove and scoot a few inches closer while trying to get just a little more rest. Luckily, the two guys I met last night, Jordan and Kenyon, brought firewood up to the tower last night. They had it nice and toasty in here a few hours ago. They're still passed out. *I wonder if they even feel the cold in their zero-degree bags.* Ha! I was feeling so proud about how lightweight my quilt was last night. I guess I get what I deserve!

I can only close my eyes for 10 minutes at a time. I have to keep tending to the fire with the small pieces of wood left over from last night burning out so quickly. I can still see my breath inside the lookout tower, even with the fire going.

Around 3:30 a.m., I step outside the tower to pee. The wind is roaring. It tries to rip the door out of my hands as I step outside. There's a latch on the inside that's been keeping the door shut with all this wind. *Is this door going to fly open when I let go of it? I don't see an outside latch.* All of a sudden, the wind catches my hat-headlamp combo and blows it off the side of the lookout tower and off the side of the peak. Fortunately, since my headlamp is on, I can see where it landed. It's not too far away and still seems to be in a fairly safe-to-access location. I'll only have to climb down a couple of steep ledges to get to it.

I step back inside, grab my phone for another form of light, and run down the stairs. The cold is blistering. My teeth chatter uncontrollably. Navigating the ledge, I snatch my hat and headlamp and sprint back toward the lookout tower. I shiver as I relieve myself before clambering back up the wooden steps. *Pee with the wind, Nick, not into it.*

Once I'm back inside the tower, I add more wood to the fire, bundle up in my quilt, and check the weather again. It's now 25 degrees at the base of the mountain. Rain, snow, and freezing temperatures are in the forecast for the remaining four days of the trip. *This is insane. I don't think it's safe to go down the mountain right now. It could be negative outside with this wind chill.* I don't know what to do. *I wish I had warmer gear.* I text Hannah to give her an update. She works her magic and finds a small hunting and outdoors store in Eureka, my next town for resupply, which is only 37 miles away. *Maybe I can buy some gloves and a rainsuit there.* It's day 25. I'm already sore and exhausted, and I haven't even started hiking yet. I decide to stay in the tower at least until the sun comes up.

My stomach is rumbling. The hunger is real. The only food I have left from my Feist Creek Resort makeshift resupply is a few chocolate bars and a couple of Mountain House-style meals. I've been holding off on eating these dehydrated meals because of the hassle. I didn't bring a stove to save space, weight, and time. I intended to cold soak these meals today. But now that I'm in this lookout tower, I have a way to cook! I use Jordan's stove to boil some water. I rehydrate the chicken fried rice and munch on a Milky Way. The hot meal and fire begin to warm me. I crack open the Coors Banquet the hunter gave me yesterday. What a way to start the day. Beer, warm food, and... my legs aren't moving. Pure bliss.

An hour later, I'm cooking dehydrated chili and eating another chocolate bar while continuing to tend to the fire. The firewood is almost gone. The sun is almost up. It's time to get moving soon.

Down Mount Henry, a quick skip by Purcell Summit, through Gypsy Meadows, over Boulder Mountain Pass, up Thirsty Mountain, over Webb Mountain, and eventually down to the Kootenai Reservoir—the trail reenters civilization. When I make it to Eureka, I stumble into Cafe Jax, a local and a PNT favorite. After eating three full entrees with sides, I'm nearly in a food coma.

Next up, gear to help me through this cold front. With my stiff legs, overstuffed belly, and aching feet—I wobble through the outdoors store. I buy a $20 rainsuit, an emergency poncho, some hand warmers, and a pair of gloves.

I cross my fingers as I approach the UPS store. I'm a day early. My box isn't supposed to arrive till tomorrow. But according to the internet, it's already here! I don't celebrate till I have it securely in my hands, though. We know what happened with my last resupply box.

My left shin muscles are astonishingly swollen and tight. I can't lift my foot by the ankle at all anymore. The toes on my left foot are tingling, going numb. *Is my ankle swelling up so much it's pinching the nerves in my toes?* I look like Frankenstein walking down the side of the road. My pace is down to less than two miles an hour. *This isn't working.*

Hannah tells me to stay in a hotel if it's going to be too cold tonight. Maybe I should, not because of the cold, but because of my leg and ankle. I can soak it in a hot bath and get a good night's rest on a warm, comfy bed. I take a look at the map. A motel is just up ahead, but I've only gone 38 miles today. *You're not even going to finish at this rate if something doesn't change, Nick.*

I check into the motel. That's motel with an "M," not hotel with an "H." It's the kind of motel that's attached to a gas station, and you check in with the gas station clerk. But it's right off the trail, right off the road the trail follows, and that's all that matters to me. I don't have to go out of my way to get to it.

After dropping my gear in my room, I hobble back to the gas station. It's time to go grocery shopping.

I fill up my motel room ice bucket with ice from the soda fountain machine and limp up and down all four aisles. Full-size bag of SunChips. Funyuns. Snickers. Sandwich. Fries. Bottle of Advil. Dr Pepper. Mountain Dew. Lemonade. *And... alcohol. I need alcohol. I'm going to knock these muscles out and make them relax.* Make that a Mike's Hard Lemonade six-pack. And some beer. Might as well grab these muffins and this burrito too.

It takes me several trips to the checkout counter to pile up my winnings. I feel like I've hit the jackpot, this hotel being connected to this gas station.

I shamble back to my room and start up the bath water. *Wish I had Epsom salt.*

Looking at myself in the mirror without my shirt on, I can see how much weight I've lost. My collar bones are defined and pronounced. Sharp. Edgy. My arms are skinny. My gut is gone. I'm not the skinny runner type to begin with, so the changes seem distinct.

I soak in the bath for an hour. It's almost too hot at first. I have to let it cool off before I get in. The hot water is painful to my feet, but the intense heat soaks deep into my legs and makes it worth it. My legs loosen and my shoulders untense. My aches go away. The water quickly darkens. I haven't even scrubbed yet. I haven't had any form of bathing since I dipped in Swan Lake 400 miles ago, and it shows.

After I climb out of the bath, I start to regret it. My feet swell up. My ankles get tighter. I can barely even walk while holding on to the bed to cross the room. With each step, I can feel the pressure in each foot rippling out from the point of contact and spreading across the rest of my feet. *Did the hot soak do this? How in the world am I supposed to finish these last 135 miles? I shouldn't have done that.*

I grab the bucket of ice, dump half of it into a trash bag, tie off the end, lie down on the bed, and place the ice bag on my shin. It rolls off to the side. I grab a couple of pillows and place them under my foot, making the center of the pillow dip down under the weight to form a cradle. Now the ice bag stays on top of my shin and ankle. Plus, my leg is elevated. Now I wait 20 minutes.

A South Park episode later, I'm taking the ice off. Another South Park episode goes by, and the ice goes back on. I religiously ice my shin on and off every 23 minutes, occasionally falling asleep, for the next four hours. *If my shin and ankle are still giving me issues in the morning, it's not going to be for lack of effort.*

As I'm icing my leg I go through my resupply box and repack my bag. I must have left my cork ball in the Mount Henry lookout tower, because it's not here. I've lost so many pieces of gear on this trip. Come to think of it, where's Encore's rain kilt he let me borrow? *Dang it… I've lost that too.*

Only 135 more miles to go. Just three more days.

THREE MORE DAYS

I'M OUT OF THE MOTEL and headed down the highway at 4:05 a.m. in my high-dollar rainsuit. It's not raining, but it's warmer than my loincloth. Thank goodness that rest did some good. I can actually walk again.

I keep checking the weather forecast, hoping it's changed. But it hasn't, and doesn't. A cold, wintery mix in the high alpine areas is headed my way for the next three days. It'll be with me till I finish the trail. It's 32 degrees out right now, and I'm not even in the mountains—I'm still in Eureka. The higher I climb, the colder it's going to be. *I'd better camp at low elevations from here on out.*

Within six miles, my rain pants have shredded in the crotch. They didn't even last until I could use them in the rain. The edges of the torn plastic are uncomfortable to my nether regions, to say the least. I take them off and stuff them in my bag. *Piece of junk.* Now I'm just carrying extra weight.

While doing my homework before I lose cell service for the next three days, I discover the fire closure near Glacier National Park has been rescinded, so I get to take the primary route through the Whitefish Divide after all. That also means I added on three miles to make up for the difference at the beginning of the PNT for nothing.

Miles go by. Time passes. The trail approaches the border of Canada. It's obvious on the map, not so much in person. If it weren't for signs, you'd never know another country was just a few feet away.

Around the backside of some bushes at the end of the northernmost switchback, I find a sign for the 49th parallel. I hop across to the other side, say hello to all of Canada, and then jump back to the US. *I'm such a rebel.*

Keep moving.

The higher I climb, the colder it gets. Once I pass 6,300 feet, there's ice on the ground—a mixture of water on the ground that froze overnight and snow that fell afterward.

Coming up over the pass below Green Mountain, I'm hit with the views of the Blue Bird Basin and beyond. *Ah… the mountains of Montana.* I've never seen these mountains from this specific viewpoint, but they have that never-ending Big Sky feel of Montana. It's the kind of view that led me to fall in love with mountains and hiking.

Tall, jagged peaks in the background take on a hint of blue, fronted by slightly gentler mountains covered in blankets of green trees. The view of the Rockies extends for what must be a hundred miles. I can't get my eyes off them. *Is that Glacier National Park, or is that Canada?* I'm too caught up in the glory of the view to check the map or compass to know for sure. It's mesmerizing. I feel like I'm coming home.

I'm lifted with energy. I start running through green conifers sprinkled with yellow larches. Every now and then, when I reach the top of a pass, the trees open up enough to catch another glimpse of the basin. These could be my favorite views of the trip so far. They could just be extra special to me because I'm nearing the finish line.

I lean down to hurdle myself over a blowdown, one arm on the tree, while jumping and tossing the rest of my body over to the other side.

Snap!

The buckle on the top sternum strap of my backpack breaks under the extra pressure of me leaning forward to get over the tree. *That's OK, I'll just wrap the strap and broken buckle around this part like this… and… there we go. Secured.* It dawns on me that this is the first piece of equipment failure I've had other than shoes or gaiters. And shoes are inevitable; shoes just don't last thousands of miles. *Wait, never mind, half my tent stakes broke too.* But seriously—if this is all that breaks on this trip, especially with all this bushwhacking, I'll consider myself blessed. *Heck, who am I kidding? I am blessed. I'm on the PNT.*

I come to a four-way junction. My map only indicates a three-way junction. I need to go straight, but my options are slightly left or slightly right. It appears that I should go right, so I start off in that direction. I check my GPS a couple of minutes into the path, and it still looks like I'm headed the right way, so I put my phone away and keep trekking along.

Before I know it, I come across another trail junction. *Wait. I shouldn't be at another junction this quickly.* I check the map. I've gone off track. *Seriously? I should have gone straight left, not straight right.* I hustle my way back up to the top of the saddle and get back on the trail. *Would I have missed that turn if I were fresh? Am I too tired? Would anyone have missed that turn?*

I start brainstorming the finish. This morning it was my intention to sleep two more nights. Tonight on the Whitefish Divide, 43 miles for the day, just before a 15-mile alpine ridgeline to avoid camping where it'd be too cold, and then I'd spend the next night at Bowman Lake at the edge of Glacier National Park before finishing out the last day.

But—if I want to take advantage of hiking while there's no rain as long as possible, I could go ahead and crush the 15-mile ridge line tonight and set up camp around 2:00 a.m. The cold, nasty rain and snow isn't supposed to start until tomorrow morning. If I do that, then sleep for four hours, I could finish with a 24-hour, 75-mile day.

Man, that sounds good. It'd be tough, especially with my shin the way it is. But that would be a solid, strong finish.

Dang it!

Only a couple of hours have passed, and it's beginning to drizzle. It's 6:00 p.m. *It's not supposed to rain until tomorrow!* I pick up my pace as if I can outrun it.

That is the biggest pile of bear scat I've ever seen in my life. It's massive. And fresh. It's steaming. I place my size 12 foot next to the mound of digested berry poo for comparison. Yup, definitely twice the size of my foot. *That was one big grizzly that left that mess. At least I have my air horn. Not!*

I'm approaching the climb for the 15-mile ridgeline. I really want to go for the strong finish, but the rain is getting heavier. It could be icy on top of the ridge. The sun is practically down already. The tendon connecting my left foot and shin muscle is trashed. And it's getting colder, quick.

Can I make it another 15 miles in dark, cold, wet, icy rain? What if I keep going and get caught in a snowstorm? It's already raining down here. That means it could already be snowing up there. What if I have to stop and sleep on top of the ridge? It'd be cold. Real cold. It wouldn't be good sleep. And I need good sleep.

And if I wait, if I sleep on this side of the mountain tonight and get up early, I can watch the sunrise as I cross over the divide. If I continue on tonight, I won't get a chance to truly experience it.

I choose the sunrise. The easier version. The safer choice. *I'll stop at the trail camp at the base of the climb. Get as close as I can before I head up in the morning.*

My shin, running all the way down to the top of my left foot, is absolutely killing me. My right hamstring is tightening up. My toes on both feet are tingly and numb. I have the opposite of a healthy gait.

Setting up camp in the rain is always fun. I quickly get under my tarp and start going through my nightly routine. *You know, I'm only like two miles from where that giant bear turd was.* The imagination can be fascinating. *That scat was really fresh too.* I lie there, imagining a giant grizzly sniffing outside my tarp, while I'm further comforted by the presence of my nonexistent air horn.

Just two more days. Just two more days.

Wait. Isn't the Whitefish Divide area where those hunters got attacked by that grizzly bear last year? Probably not. (But it is.) I have nothing to worry about. I've had well over 50 bear encounters in the last two years, and I've never felt threatened. *Well, except for that one bear near Bowman Lake that was really pissed off a year ago. Ha! That trail is part of the PNT too. I'll be passing by that same spot in less than 48 hours.*

Just two more days.

SAVING THE BEST FOR LAST

WELL. I DIDN'T GET EATEN by a bear last night. I'm still alive.

I quickly pack up. It's not raining anymore. *Thank you.*

Just two more days.

Up toward Mount Locke I climb. I don't see any stars. The clouds must still be thick, blocking the sky, preparing to rain for the next two days until I finish the trail.

It's cool out. I'm moving faster than I'd expect considering how wrecked my left leg is. The higher I climb, the more snow and ice I find on the ground. The vegetation crowding out the trail is bitter cold and wet. As I walk through the overgrown brush, the frigid water hits my legs. I'm not so concerned about my feet getting wet anymore. In fact, I'm thankful. The ice-cold water is numbing the pain.

Just two more days.

I reach the top of the ridge and an opening in the trees. The sun is beginning to rise. Purples, pinks, blues. A long valley perfectly aligned with my view, with mountains gently sloping up either side. Silhouettes of perfectly symmetrical evergreens up close provide depth. Without a doubt, it's the best sunrise of the entire trip. It could be the best sunrise of my life.

OK, seriously? Stop it. This view is insane. I keep stopping dead in my tracks to stare at it and take a picture every time the trees open to give a view of the valley. *I'm so glad I waited for the sunrise.* It's a magical moment. One of those sunrises that you don't just see. It can't be described; it has to be felt. It's like the trail was saving its best for last.

Pit stop to wring out my socks and give my feet some air time. Vegetation isn't crowding out the trail on top of this ridge. Might as well dump some water while I can sit and watch the sunrise at the same time.

Twenty minutes later: *Where the hell are my Starbursts?* They must have fallen out of my pocket when I stopped to wring out my socks. I was really looking forward to those. Hannah had even removed all the individual wrappers for me so I wouldn't have a bunch of excess trash on the trail.

I'm leaving a trail of debris behind me. Starbursts. Cork ball. Rain kilt. Headband. Microfiber towel. Burt's Bees. I know I've lost more than that. At least I haven't lost any of my sleeping gear or pertinent items for completing the trip. *I am the worst at leave no trace.*

Before I'm done with the ridgeline, it begins sleeting. The sprinkling sleet turns into a constant drizzle of wet snow. An arctic wind rushes in. A dark, nasty, freezing, wet sleet and rain persists throughout the rest of the day. I bundle up under my poncho, rain jacket, puffy jacket, long sleeve, and sleeveless shirt—every layer of clothing I have. I'm still cold. *Just keep moving. Just two more days.*

But the views make up for it. It's a rush of beauty combined with a rollercoaster of emotions. I'm having the time of my life, while at the same time I'm miserably cold and numb. *Move faster and you'll get warmer.*

I start running. It's fun. The trees are spaced out; there are plenty of open, majestic views. I'm excited to see what's around each corner, driving me through the ups and downs as the trail follows 15 miles of jaw-dropping alpine beauty across the Whitefish Divide.

After the ridge, I'm back on forest service roads and trails that used to be forest service roads. Some of them were decommissioned so long ago there are trees growing in the middle. Road to trail, and trail back to road. I haven't seen anyone for days.

There's no one out here. So, of course, my shorts aren't on. They are hanging from my backpack sternum strap, barely low enough to provide some kind of coverage in an emergency situation. Plus, it's still raining, so I'm using my new poncho rain jacket combo. My lower half is covered by a clear poncho and the sliver of my shorts that happen to hang low enough in the front. Full moon shining in the back.

All of a sudden, there's an old red truck headed straight for me. There's nothing to hide behind. It's too late to attempt putting my shorts back on. My best option is to pull the corner of shorts that are hanging from my sternum strap down farther and hold it in place like a matador's flag for some coverage. *They'll be past me and on their way soon enough.*

Or so I thought.

The truck slows to an idle.

The driver rolls his window down.

He stops beside me. "Does this road go all the way through to Eureka?"

"No. It stops about a mile ahead. I just got off of a hiking trail onto it."

"Our map says this road keeps going over these mountains and connects with another one on the other side."

"Well… it doesn't. Where my trail ended, this road began. The trail was an old road at one point but has since been decommissioned and turned into a hiking trail. This is a dead-end road now."

"Our map shows this road we are on as a solid white line, and it continues straight over the mountain. It turns into a black line soon, but we were told we could make it all the way across."

"That black line is probably where this road turns into the trail." *How have they not noticed I'm not wearing any pants?* We're arguing about a road while I'm practically naked. I'm still holding my shorts down from my sternum strap; they are barely long enough to cover anything up. Maybe the clear poncho is somehow helping?

"OK, I guess we are turning around. I'm going to do a U-turn up here."

I've gotta get my shorts back on ASAP. They pull forward about 25 feet and start to turn around. I sit down on the ground before they can see my pasty-white cheeks and slide into my shorts, hoping they are concentrating on their turn and not looking at me.

My shorts are on. I'm back to walking. And they seem to be struggling with making what must be a 12-point turn. Eventually, they catch back up. They slow down as they pass by and roll down a window again. The guy asks with a country accent, "Yer not runnin' from the law or anything out here, are ye'?"

"No. I'm hiking the Pacific Northwest Trail." I'm laughing to myself inside. How in the world has he not commented about me not wearing pants just a moment ago, but he's asking if I'm running from the police? Do naked people run from the police a lot where he's from or something?

The truck drives off, and I eventually make it to the Polebridge Mercantile, a small off-grid trading post the size of a convenience store. It's an escape from the rain. I buy four giant huckleberry brownies, a bear claw, apple fritter, four cans of Dr Pepper, a couple of slices of pizza, and a banana. They hand it all to me in a full-size brown paper grocery sack. It's too big to fit in my pack.

I limp down the dirt road in the rain, holding said grocery sack like a baby, talking to it softly, hunched over to protect it from the elements.

I've already eaten one slice of pizza, have the second slice in my right hand and the paper sack cradled in my left arm. After the pizza is gone, I keep reaching in, meticulously choosing what I'll eat next. I have so many fresh options. *I'm saving one of these brownies for Hannah, though.*

When I get to Bowman Lake, I have two choices. Keep going and camp on the other end, or camp right here in one of these easily available campsites that don't require a backcountry permit—because I don't have one. If I go to the other end of the lake tonight, I'll have to cross my fingers on getting a permit at the Ranger Station, and I doubt they are even still open today.

I opt for one of the easily available, no-permit-required, first-come-first-serve campsites near the parking lot. It's funny to look at my tiny little tarp taking up this tiny little space. The campsite is big enough for an entire family, multiple cars, even a camper trailer, and a week's worth of car camping gear—and I'm taking up a six-foot by four-foot corner.

As I munch on brownies and a bear claw, I go through my gear. *Tomorrow is the last day. What can I get rid of?* I make a pile to haul over to the trash can. Shredded piece of junk rainsuit. Haven't used these hand warmers; they go too. I don't need this Leuko tape. Don't need this; don't need that. Don't need this foot powder; I'll use the rest in the morning and toss it. *Wait.* I shake the bottle. *I've used an entire full-size bottle of foot powder in a week?* And I'll just throw away my groundsheet in the morning too.

I finish eating all the food in my sack except for two brownies. One for Hannah and the other for me tomorrow afternoon. I stuff my trash pile in the now empty paper sack. The once empty sack is now full again.

As I hobble over to the trash can in the dark, I think about tomorrow. The last day. Should I start at midnight instead of 4:00 a.m.? Last year, when I was in Glacier, near Brown Pass, I saw five grizzlies and a black bear all within five miles of each other. I'll be going through that part in the dark tomorrow morning. Per reports, it's overgrown and bushy still. Running through overgrowth, in the dark, in an area with high grizzly bear traffic, with no form of bear protection? *That's real smart, Nick. Real smart.*

I compromise. I'll start at 2:00 a.m. The sun should be coming up by the time I get to Brown Pass, so it won't be quite as sketchy.

CHARIOTS OF FIRE

TODAY'S DAY 28, the final day. Only it's actually day 27. I've been counting day one as day one, when in reality, 24 hours doesn't hit until day two. Day one should be day zero. So I've been thinking I'm on pace to finish the trail in sub 29 days, when I'm actually about to do it in sub 28.

The excitement to finish wakes me up several times in the night. I'm restless. I eventually start the day at 2:00 a.m., but I regret not starting sooner. *You should have just started moving the first time you woke up.* I'm thankful it's not raining anymore, though. *At least I get to start the last day off dry.*

This is the lightest my pack has been. All my food is in front shoulder strap pockets or in my waist belt. Glacier National Park is full of mountain streams, so I only have a half-liter of water on me. It's cold, so I'm wearing all my layers. All that's inside my bag are my quilt, sleeping pad, bivy, and tarp. It's weightless. I feel agile again.

Just one more day. Just cross Glacier National Park, and you're done. Just one more day.

I come across a bear warning sign: "High bear activity around Brown Pass." *I bet it's the same bears I saw last year.* I wonder if I'll see the same five grizzlies. It is somewhat close to the same time of year.

It's not raining, but I'm already wet. Moving through soggy, over-grown vegetation seems to get you wet faster than rain does. It's so cold. I bring my arms inside the emergency poncho I picked up in Eureka, trying to keep them at least a little drier and a little warmer than if they were brushing up against all the ice-cold overgrowth too.

I lean forward, pull the poncho hood down, and wrap my arms tight. I've turned myself into a waterproof bulldozer to plow through the underbrush.

Once I get to the far side of Bowman Lake and start climbing up in elevation toward Brown Pass it starts raining, and I start clapping my hands while yelling, "Hey bear!"

Normally, I'm the silent hiker. I want to see the wildlife. I want to see their majesty. Trust me when I say I want to see the animals. It annoys me when I hear bear bells or other hikers clapping and yelling, "Hey bear." But not today. Today I just want to finish, and I don't want to spook any grizzlies that might be hiding on the other side of one of these bushes in the dark.

"Heyyyyyyy bear." "Hey beeeeeaaaaar." "Heyyyy beeeaaarrrr."

I'm singing it now. OK, I'm having way too much fun with this "hey bear" stuff. I'm trotting along by myself in the woods, with a tiny little backpack, in the rain, in the middle of the dark, singing, "Hey bear. Hey bear." *No bear is going to want to mess with this crazy fool.*

The rain turns to light snow once I reach the alpine.

By the time I'm on Brown Pass, the sun is up. I stop. Take a deep breath. And soak it in. This is where I fell in love with big miles. This is what led me to where I am today. In fact, this is the exact spot where I first heard of the PNT—when I bumped into a PNT hiker last year. But this is as far as I've gone.

The other side of the pass is rugged, cloudy, and majestic—just as Glacier always is—but it has its own story to tell. *How is every valley out here different, yet still completely "Glacier National Park"?*

Deep 'U'-shaped valleys, carved by ancient glacial flow, lie in front of me. *The finish line is just over that line of mountains.* Well, behind the line of mountains that are behind that line of mountains. And by "just over," I mean 36 miles away.

I was expecting clean trail conditions at least some of the way through Glacier. National parks are usually well maintained. What was I thinking? This is the PNT. The trails are WAY overgrown, and everything is wet. It's hard to run. I can barely see the trail at my feet through the thick leaves.

Just keep moving.

With my hands pulled inside my poncho, I discover I can easily operate my phone screen for GPS navigation in the rain. The poncho is a windshield. *Whhhhaaaaaaat?*

My biggest struggle of the entire trip—navigating through overgrown areas in the rain and not being able to operate my GPS screen because it's wet—could have been completely eliminated if I just pulled my hands inside a poncho? My mind is blown. *Way to figure that out on the last day, Nick.*

I keep moving. Keep trucking forward. I've been walking the majority of the day; I can't find a rhythm to run with on these overgrown trails. Or maybe I'm just worn out.

Soon the PNT connects with the Continental Divide Trail (CDT). The PNT travels along three scenic long trails, so I've been getting a taste of each one. The Pacific Crest Trail in Washington. The Idaho Centennial Trail in—you guessed it—Idaho. And the Continental Divide Trail right here in Montana. I run into a few CDT hikers finishing their journey from Mexico to Canada. *That's got to feel good. I'm finishing up 1,248 miles; I can only imagine 3,000.* They don't even know what the PNT is. It makes me laugh.

I think about how many people I've seen on this short section of the CDT. I think about how many people I saw on the 14 miles along the PCT. Are these trails this crowded all the time? I've practically had the entire PNT to myself outside of Olympic National Park and a handful of other places. I've enjoyed the solitude. You really get to connect with a trail by having it all to yourself.

As I'm climbing up Stoney Indian Pass, I'm eating the last of my food. *After this granola bar, all I have left is Hannah's brownie.* I check the map, something that seems to be habitual by now. I'm always checking the map. The top of Stoney Indian Pass is mile 1,230. Mile

1,248 is the end. I have 18 miles to go once I finish this climb and no food left. My stomach is already rumbling.

I'm sorry, Hannah. I pull her brownie out. I'll savor it. Eat it slowly. Maybe I'll have half of it left for her when I reach the end.

At the top of the pass, I'm taking the last bite of the brownie. It's like it just disintegrated once it was in front of my mouth. *How are you supposed to eat a brownie that tastes this good, slowly?*

The view coming down Stoney Indian Pass opens, allowing me to see straight down the Belly River Valley. Across multiple lakes, just under 18 miles away now, is Hannah. She's in a parking lot somewhere on top of that hill at the end of the valley. It's as if I can see the end, literally.

It starts to sleet. I start to run.

It's a downhill, easy, cruisey slope from here until the small hill at the end. I turn on the GPS tracker on my watch so I can see exactly what my pace is. I don't need to reserve battery anymore. I don't need to reserve energy either. If I hustle, I might be able to finish before the sun sets.

The run down is invigorating. *How is this happening?* I'm having fun, running at an 8.5-minute-per-mile pace, while my body is completely trashed.

I maintain the pace, stopping only to take a few photos to remember the moment by. *Just 12 more miles. Just eight more miles. Just six more miles.*

All of a sudden Guthooks, my primary map, has stopped working. It's logged me out and is saying I need an internet connection to log back in. *What the hell?* I try entering my login name and password. It doesn't work. I don't have cell service.

You have got to be kidding me.

I completely close the app. Reopen it. Close it. Reopen it. Somehow hoping that just constantly closing out of the app and reopening it will make it work. I restart my phone. Still doesn't work. I don't have a paper map with me for Glacier. It's a national park. Their trail junctions are always well-marked, so I didn't figure I'd need one when planning everything out. Surely there's no way I'll take a wrong turn out here. Besides that, it's just six more miles. *But this is the PNT…*

Just keep moving.

When I reach the last 1.8 miles, the climb up the hill to the Chief Mountain Trailhead goes by quicker than I expect it to. Suddenly, I see the roofs of a few cars. I see a clearing in the trees where a parking lot must be. I start to run again. *Where's the sign? Where's the sign?!*

I don't see the sign!!

Boom. There it is: the Chief Mountain Trailhead sign. I run up to it, snap a photo next to the PNT emblem, and turn off my InReach tracker.

The timer has stopped.

I'm done.

I head up the 15-foot hill to the parking lot and walk toward the middle, away from the parking spots, toward the middle of the aisle. I'm looking for Hannah.

There's the car! As soon as I spot it, Hannah opens the driver's door and steps outside. She runs toward me. We hug. We kiss. And then I collapse.

As soon as my body knew I was done, it was done.

OK, OK, so I didn't actually collapse and crumble to the ground. I just sat down so fast it was as if I collapsed. It was one of those situations where I knew I could keep standing if I wanted to, but I *really* didn't want to. I didn't want to be on my feet anymore. I wanted to sit. I wanted to lie down. I wanted to rest.

And so I sit there in the middle of the asphalt and take my shoes, socks, and pack off. Hannah runs back to the car to grab her phone to take a photo, to document the end. She comes over, leans down behind me, and takes a selfie. With her arms wrapped around me, I can finally relax. I'm safe. I'm done. I don't have to fend for myself anymore. I don't have to walk. I'm finally back with the one person I can be my true self with, without putting on a face. She doesn't judge me. She doesn't try to change me. She accepts me, no matter how trashed I am and no matter how bad I stink. The last time I saw her was 27 days, 13 hours, and 32 minutes ago. It's a double win—finishing the trail and getting to be with her again.

I start crawling toward the car across the pavement. It's only 30 feet away. I'm on my hands and knees; I don't want my feet to touch the ground. I don't want my ankles to have to bend. They're done. They get a break. This is the least I can do for my feet after they've carried me this far.

On all fours, I keep inching forward. Only 20 more feet to go. I've gone from FKT on the PNT to SKT on the PLT (Slowest Known Time on the Parking Lot Trail).

I keep crawling. And Hannah starts humming Chariots of Fire.

It's Hannah's version of welcoming me home. And I dig it.

THE AFTER

MY FEET ARE FAT. Ankles are fat. Legs are stiff.

Hannah shows me the cooler. It's stocked with all kinds of juice, lemonade, Gatorade, and Dr Pepper. She gives me a pair of size 14 slippers to get around in until my feet come back down to normal size. She sets out the scale so I can weigh myself. I've lost 26.6 pounds while eating 8,000 calories a day.

We leave the Chief Mountain Trailhead by car—it feels odd to be in a car. Hours away from any reasonable hotel, we drive through the flats of Montana on the east side of the Continental Divide. Nothing but flat to the east, and nothing but the rugged peaks of Glacier National Park to the west. It's barely been half an hour, and I can't get comfortable.

I put my feet on the dashboard, trying to elevate them for some kind of relief. A few minutes pass. *OK, that's not going to work.* I put them back on the floorboard of the car and twist my body for a different angle. Back up on the dash. Back to the floor. Off to the side. Let's try twisting again. I grab pillows and blankets. I can't get comfy.

"Everything hurts and I'm dying." - Leslie Knope, *Parks and Rec.*

The longer I sit, the more time that passes—the worse the swelling gets and the worse the pain gets.

Hannah finds us a hotel. I don't even know where we're at. All I know is she looked up the closest hotels with a pool. If there's a pool, there's likely a hot tub. *Oh, if I could just soak in a hot tub, maybe, just maybe, some of these aches would go away.*

She walks in and gets us a room. She parks in the closest parking spot to the front door as possible. I inch my way toward the front, waddle through the hotel lobby, and we start working our way down the hall. We don't have to go very far. Hannah asked for the closest room to the foyer, so we're in room one. It's the first guest room we'll come across. But I swear this is the longest walk of my life. *Should have ridden in the luggage cart.*

We walk past the pool room. It has glass walls. You can see the entire swim setup, but there's no hot tub. Hannah's apologizing, "Sorry! I really thought his hotel had a hot tub." I don't even care at this point. I just want to lie down. I can soak in the bathtub once we get to the room anyway.

Hannah opens our hotel room door. I step inside, and we look in the bathroom. *There's no bathtub.* This is a handicap room. It's a handicap shower with handrails and a fold-down bench to sit on. I still don't care. At least there's a bench.

I immerse myself under the running water. I sit there, not wanting to move. Not wanting to scrub. Not wanting to lather up. I just sit and relax for what must be an hour.

When I get out of the shower and eventually make it to the bed, Hannah fills an empty trash can with hot water, Epsom salts, and essential oils. She's making me a foot soak.

It hurts. I thought the foot soak would feel good. But my feet are in so much pain. It's a good pain, though. One of those aches that's supposed to make you feel better in the end.

By the next day, my feet and ankles double in size. It's like once I stopped moving, they became balloons—slowly inflating to max capacity over a 24-hour period. These size 14 slippers are coming in handy.

On our way through Denver, Hannah suggests a pedicure. I've never had one before, so I'm not really sure what to expect. Hannah says I can skip the nail polish and go straight to the foot massage and soak part. *A foot massage sounds so good.*

I hobble into a nail salon. "I just want a foot massage."

The lady at the front desk pulls out a laminated piece of paper with four pedicure options. She points to the most expensive package, "This one has an extra-long foot massage at the end." "I'm sold. I'll take it."

I'm guided to sit down in a chair with a foot bath at the bottom. I sit in the chair and wait for something to happen. *This is so weird.* I feel awkward. Out of place. A girl with one-inch-long pink fingernails, a leopard print bodysuit, and a pink cell phone case is talking on the phone two chairs over to the left. She has a valley girl accent, "Oh. Em. Gee. Like, I think I'm going to have to do something about that, but, like, I don't really want to have to do anything about it. So, I like, I don't know what to do. Do you know what I mean?"

What have I gotten myself into?

Finally, this tiny figure of a nail expert rolls over to me on a stool. She has a box full of gadgets and nail polish. "You don't have to do anything to my nails; I just want a foot massage. I just finished a long hike, and my feet hurt. I just want a soft, gentle foot massage."

She starts clipping my toenails. "No, no, no. You don't have to clip my nails. Just a foot massage."

She keeps clipping.

Does she even hear me? Does she even speak English? "Please leave my nails alone." *She doesn't understand me at all. Great.*

Luckily, she doesn't paint them. After clipping the nails, she starts shaving parts of the calluses off my heels and toes with a cheese grater. It tickles. It hurts. It's unnecessary, but I must endure. My feet are so sore. *All I wanted was a foot massage.* I just have to sit here and take it. What if I wanted that callus?

FINALLY. The foot massage begins. But it's not gentle. She just rubs the sides of my legs and ankles really fast. No caressing. No care. She's just going through the motions. Don't get me wrong, it kind of feels good. I think any massage at this point would feel somewhat good. But at the same time, it's uncomfortable. My feet and tendons around my ankles are so tender.

Here I am. My poor, pitiful, vulnerable feet in the hands of someone who can't understand me. I send Hannah a picture of the dead skin piled up on the cheese grater. She responds back with a vomit emoji and says, "Give her a $20 tip."

When we get home and I'm finally lying down in our own bed, it's so comfortable. I'm finally in a state of comfortable pain. I can finally be at peace with my pain.

I'm so glad to be done. So glad to be home. But I hurt worse than when I was on trail. I knew I was going to be wrecked, but I didn't think I was going to be this wrecked.

I wake up famished at 3:00 a.m. and crawl to the kitchen, then crawl back to bed and fall asleep with pizza in my mouth. A few days later, I progress to limping back to bed with food. I keep getting up for more sustenance every couple of hours.

Hannah brings me bacon in bed for breakfast. *Did I die? Is this heaven?*

All I'm doing is eating and sleeping. Or trying to sleep. I struggle to sleep at first. It hurts too bad to sleep. That, and I'm so hungry, I can't stay asleep. I keep waking up for more and more food. A half-gallon of ice cream in milkshakes in a day. A whole pizza followed by eight slices of cinnamon toast. I'm devouring everything in sight. Soon I have a belly again. *That didn't last long.*

I miss sleeping outside. Don't get me wrong, I'm digging this comfy king-size bed, but I miss falling asleep under the stars. I miss the cold nights, bundling up in my quilt and somehow magically becoming cozy. It feels like home under the roof of our house, but it feels weird. It's strange to brush my teeth with a full-size toothbrush. It's so heavy. So bulky. The handle is so long.

We have to wash my shorts from the PNT eight times to get them clean. Four times in the washer and four times soaking in the sink with degreaser. Hannah is eventually able to get my shirt mostly back to white.

The next week I need to get out of the house. I can't take it anymore. I'm so sick of being cooped up inside, but I still can't walk normally. *Home Depot!* They have those electric wheelchair carts. And so I'm riding around the home improvement store in a motorized shopping cart. Up and down the aisles. Backing up. Turning around. Doing 360s. *These little carts have an excellent turn radius.*

A couple of weeks after the PNT, I'm finally moving around on a more regular basis. I'm still not walking right, but I'm not handicapped anymore. I start cleaning and putting away my PNT gear. I see the maps of the PCT on the walls in my gear room. This is where I did most of my planning for the PCT—the planning that prepared me for the PNT. *Hmmm...* I look at the maps some more. *Nope, there's no way. There's no way I could have gone twice as far.* The PCT is twice the distance of the PNT. How could I have gone twice as far with how wrecked I am? It's been two weeks since I finished, and I still can't walk without looking like I've been hit by a truck.

Almost four weeks pass after finishing the trail before I'm able to walk with ease again. I'm still a little stiff when I first get moving after a long break, but I don't feel debilitated. I find myself running across the house without even realizing it. *Wait... I just ran up the stairs...* "Hannah!!! Did you hear how fast I came up the stairs?"

"No."

"I'm back to running again!"

Time moves on. My feet are healing; I can finally move. I make my way back to my gear room. I had previously committed to doing some trail maintenance on the Ouachita Trail, and it's time to pack for my first camping trip since the PNT. I start looking at the PCT maps again. Memories of the PNT start flowing through my mind while they collide with the memories from planning for the PCT. *But the PNT was gnarly. It was rugged. The PCT is clean. Could I go twice as far if the trail was clean?*

Maybe I could.

Maybe I actually could hike the PCT faster than anyone's ever done before.

And so the itching begins.

The itch for another FKT is back.

ACKNOWLEDGMENTS

Thank you to Hannah. None of this would have been possible without you. Thank you for holding down the fort, for allowing me to chase after my dreams, and for being the only person who gets me for who I am.

I can't say enough thanks to Joe McConaughy for teaching me the ins and outs of an FKT. I'm not sure I would have finished the PNT the way I did if it weren't for all the tips, tricks, and running development that Joe provided.

Thanks to Jeff Garmire for putting the PNT on the FKT board as something to go after and an even bigger thanks for writing the foreword. Cheers.

To the PNTA (Pacific Northwest Trail Association) and Ron Strickland: Thank you dearly for what you do and have done for the trail. The PNT has a special place in my heart. Thank you.

Thru-hiking fast is the closest thing to heaven on earth I've ever experienced, trail angels included. Thank you to everyone who helped me along the way. It wouldn't be the same without you.

To Christine Reed, thanks for helping with the publishing process. I would have had many regrets without your guidance.

And to my mom, Stephanie Fields: Thanks for your help in editing, adding your chapter spin, and for putting up with me as a child (and as an adult).

To the PNT: You are raw. You are wild. I wouldn't want you any other way. Don't let anyone mess you up.

Pre-readers: THANK YOU. Your insight and encouragement have been invaluable. I would have been lost without you.

And of course, what's a book without a cover? Thanks, Dave Cole.

HANNAH'S VERSION

IT ALL STARTED ONE DAY in Glacier National Park. Nick said, "Sooo, I was thinking of hiking to this glacier…" One thing you have to know about Nick is that when he starts a sentence with "Sooo, I was thinking," it typically means he's about to do something crazy.

Nick told me about this plan he had to hike approximately 22 miles to touch a couple of glaciers. We were a year into our love for the outdoors, and I could easily hike over 10 miles in a day, but 22?! No. No, thank you, sir.

I dropped him off early in the morning and planned to pick him up by dinner. I had my own formula for Nick's hike time: 20-minute miles squared to the power of "if he sees something cool, he'll get sidetracked and start exploring." Total time by my wifely calculation, plus or minus 10 hours. Since there wasn't cell service, I waited 10 minutes after watching him hike out of sight before leaving him to fend for himself.

Arlowe, our cattle dog, and I had a day of relaxation while Nick tortured his legs. We went exploring, had lunch by a lake, and read a book. When evening fell, I waited for him at the trailhead for nearly an hour. I watched other hikers come and go, but there was no sign of Nick. I figured either my timing was off or he found something else worth exploring and got distracted. I drove back to the visitor center for cell service to see if he had texted me from the top of a mountain with an update. Once I got there, still no word, so I drove back to the trailhead. I drove through the parking lot and circled the restrooms—looking to see if he had already made it back. Then I saw him. He was moving slow. Dirty and exhausted, he waved his arms high in the air to flag me down. We were reunited! And it felt so good.

As soon as I parked, he got in the van and said, "I'm so happy to see you. I could hear the van coming like a beacon." (Our old Volkswagen Vanagon has a distinct sound; you can hear it long before you can see it.) He said, "I hiked way longer than I intended. Instead of 22 miles, it was about 32." Whoa.

Once we got to our campsite, I told Nick I was going to walk Arlowe and let her go potty before we went to bed. We walked around for a few minutes and came back to the campsite to find Nick—still getting out of the front seat of the van. He was barely moving. I asked him if he was OK, and he winced, "Just a little sore." We joked about how he was going to be very sore in the morning if he was this sore now.

This is the day it all started for him—the day we laugh about often—the "accidental 32-mile day hike." From then on, he started seeking out longer hikes everywhere we went, pushing his limits to see how many miles he could hike in a day. Eventually he started running, pushing the miles even farther.

One day Nick said, "Sooo I was thinking about hiking the Pacific Crest Trail—and setting a speed record." What!? That sounds like a wild idea, very Nick. I'm in!

He quickly started self-training, and he trained hard. We were back at our home base in Oklahoma by this point. When you're used to hiking amazing mountains all over the country, Oklahoma can be a disappointment, but Nick still made it work. What a trooper. In his second month of training, he was running a marathon a day when a snowstorm with record-breaking temperatures hit. It was below zero degrees—crazy for Oklahoma! It would have slowed most people down, but Nick stayed committed to his training regardless of the conditions. It was inspiring to see his dedication and drive. He would ask me if I needed anything from the grocery store and literally run to the store with a hiking backpack and come home with it full of groceries. When we closed on our new house, we were still snowed in, so Nick ran to the next town over with our earnest money check and hand-delivered it to the title company. He did a lot of things like this to ensure he kept up with training. There were seemingly no obstacles he couldn't overcome.

Nick is a numbers guy. Anyone who knows Nick knows this about him. He had a spreadsheet of all of his gear so he could have a running total of the weight for each item. The amount of precision was comical because he literally weighed everything. Sleeping bag: 13.8 oz, backpack: 13.4 oz, socks: 2.3 oz, Snickers bar: 1.86 oz—you get the idea. When you are about to run over two thousand miles, every ounce counts. I joked about it a lot, but seeing his spreadsheet and the logic behind it—it made total sense. He had a funny obsession with lightweight gear. He kept finding lighter items to replace his current inventory. It was hilarious seeing how excited he got when he found something that was one ounce lighter than something he already had.

There was a room in our house dedicated to prep. I like to call it Nick's office, but it's really just a gear room with all things outdoors. Anything from backpacks and sleeping bags to bear canisters and a month's worth of food. It looked (and still looks) like an end-of-the-world prep room. Floor to ceiling of prep.

During his prep, I would wake up in the middle of the night to find Nick not in bed. I would go into his office in the middle of the night to see him organizing, planning, weighing, and test-packing all of his gear. Think scientist in a lab on the brink of discovery—his excitement was palpable. Sometimes I would find him fully dressed at 3:00 a.m., backpack on, gear loaded like he had just walked out of the wilderness.

Then the fires in California surrounding the PCT exploded, closing too much of the trail for an FKT attempt. Still determined for an FKT, Nick decided to hike the Pacific Northwest Trail instead. We camped on the coast of Washington, near the eastern end of the PNT, for a couple of days before he started. The night before he started, I kept waking up every hour in anticipation.

It was strange dropping him off at the trailhead the next morning. There was a small amount of unease because I was about to drop him off and drive 2,200 miles away from him, and he was about to hike over 1,200 miles on his own. I wouldn't be around the corner to save him if something went wrong. But the feeling of unease was soon replaced with excitement, because against all the obstacles he faced starting this journey, he was finally setting off to accomplish this long-awaited goal of his! The only thing keeping me grounded was the fact that he had been planning, researching, and preparing for so long. He was more than ready for this. We said our reluctant goodbyes, and he went on his way. I waited 10 minutes after dropping him off, per tradition, said a prayer for him and started my journey back to Oklahoma.

During his epic journey, I talked to him during some of the highs, lows, and frustrations—but we weren't able to talk much. Other than him not being home, the lack of communication was one of the hardest things for me. He kept his phone on airplane mode to preserve battery most of the time, but when he did have it on, the cell service was spotty. It sucked. Sometimes he would call me from the top of a mountain, but he'd lose service within a couple of sentences.

Time went quickly. It felt like I had just dropped him off when it was suddenly time to start driving to Montana to pick him up. When I tell you I packed all the things, I packed ALL. THE. THINGS. Anything and everything I thought he would need for our 1,600-mile drive home. I mean, the guy just trekked over 1,200 miles across three states; he needed supplies. I packed pillows, blankets, recovery sandals, shoes, and a change of clean clothes. Oils and Epsom salts for a foot soak. Toiletries, a beard trimmer, Biofreeze. The cooler was packed to the brim with juice, lemonade, Red Bull (sorry, Mom), and Dr Pepper.

When it came time to pick him up, I had a general idea of when he'd arrive but figured he'd either be absolutely exhausted and moving slow—or sprinting toward the finish line at full speed. It was cold out. I remember thinking, "Nick has to be freezing out here in shorts and a sleeveless shirt!" I waited in the warm car for a while before deciding to get out of the car to keep an eye out for him. When I opened the car door, he was there—standing in the middle of the parking lot—dirty, stinky, and happy. VICTORY!!!

It was so exciting to be there to see him cross the finish line and become the new record holder! After nearly a month—27 days, 13 hours, and 32 minutes, to be exact—it was amazing to see him. I ran to him; we hugged and kissed and said our hellos, then he immediately sat down. I said something like, "Oh no, no, no. Why don't you sit in the car? Once you sit down, it's going to be hard to get up." But it was too late. His body was already cooling down. He took off his bag, his shoes and socks, and lay down in the middle of the parking lot. I leaned down next to him and took a picture to document his victory. I started loading his gear in the car, and from a sitting position, he very slowly rolled to his side to begin to stand. Or so I thought. Instead, all he could do was crawl on all fours toward the car. In that split second, I thought to myself, "What do I, the loving wife, do in this situation? Help him up, right?" Of course! But first, a video—because that's what Nick would do. So I started recording. The Chariots of Fire song came to mind, so that's what I hummed for 15 seconds before helping him up. About 10 minutes later, we got him in the car—another victory.

I put his shoes, socks, and dirty clothes in a bag. Imagine the same shorts and shirt for 27 days without being washed—the smell—wow.

Normally we don't like spending money on hotels, but after this journey, a hotel stay was required. I checked us in, grabbed all our clothes and supplies, and found the closest parking spot to the door because my 1,200-mile-running husband could barely walk. I lent him a shoulder, and we started making our way inside. It must have taken us ten minutes just to get to room number one, the closest room to the front door. After the longest shower he'd ever taken, he slept like the dead.

We weren't in a rush the next morning, but we made sure to get up for breakfast. When Nick and I do stay in a hotel, we make sure to take full advantage of anything we can. You can't turn down free, aka already paid for with the hotel price, breakfast. We were a short walk, maybe four to five doors down from the breakfast room, but it took us several minutes to get there. Nick leaned on me, and we shuffled our way down. After breakfast, we joked about needing a wheelchair to wheel him back to the room. Nick then looked at me with a face only Nick can give and said, "The chair in our hotel room has wheels." You bet we did it. I wheeled that chair down the hall to pick him up, and we rolled back to our room in style. The looks we got were comical, but no apologies.

Nick's feet and legs were in so much pain he couldn't even drive on the way back home. His feet were too swollen to even fit in his shoes, so he hobbled around in slippers. He was a sight to see, knee-high compression socks, size 14 slippers, and shuffling like a 100-year-old. HOT.

Recovery was a B. You would think after a month on your feet, recovery would be bliss, but no, it wasn't. If you know Nick, you know he has a hard time sitting still for too long. Even after running across three states, after a few days, his mind was restless and ready for his body to be back to normal. He was on bed rest for nearly a week, crawling to the bathroom and kitchen. He was consuming So. Much. Food. When you are used to eating 8,000 calories a day, your body has a hard time adjusting to life off the trail quickly. After a week, Nick graduated from crawling to shuffling. I like to call it his zombie walk. You know *The Walking Dead* zombies? That's about how Nick moved for the next three weeks. It was well over a month before he was walking pre-FKT normal. I remember one day he ran up the stairs and came straight to my office and said, "Did you hear that?" To which I replied, "Hear what?" He then said, "Did you hear how fast I ran up the stairs?" This guy, he's got jokes.

A few weeks after that, Nick came up to me and said, "Sooo, I was thinking…"

Can't wait to see where our next adventure will take us!

NICK'S MOM'S PERSPECTIVE

IT DOESN'T SURPRISE ME in the least that Nick got an FKT on his first thru-hike. Not just because I'm his mom and happen to think he's pretty great, but because there were signs from the beginning that he wasn't just the usual kid. Nick has always been uncommonly driven, determined, focused and curious. When he was a toddler, his nick-name that our community knew him and called him by was "Danger Nick."

Once, when he was a toddler playing in the backyard, I looked out the window (I was washing dishes) and noticed that I couldn't see him playing in the sandbox. He had just been there moments ago. I went out to check on him. I couldn't find him. I ran to check the gate. It was still closed. Our fence was six feet tall. I started to panic. I ran up and down the street looking for him. Had someone abducted him? I was screaming his name and knocking on all the neighboring doors to ask if they had seen him. (Thank goodness this story has a happy ending.) The child had scaled the six-foot fence to go exploring the woods behind our yard. He wasn't even out of diapers yet!

Soon after, I spent a day at our church, preparing lessons for Mother's Day Out and Sunday School class. I had kept Nick and his sister, Jill, in my room all day. All I had to do next was turn in my key and we were headed home. Within that five-minute time frame, the custodian came asking, "Whose kid is this? I found him hanging off the basketball goal saying, "Need help. Need help." Yep, you guessed it. That "kid" was Nick. He was two and a half years old. Hanging from the basketball goal rim.

Then, when he was three, he climbed a tower of jumbled furniture, toys, sports equipment and miscellaneous stuff in the church storage closet to get a ball. He climbed all the way to the top of a two-story closet and accidentally hit his head on the bare light bulb. The glass broke and he electrocuted himself. He fell the whole way down and smelled like burning hair. His hair had actually melted together and was still smoking. We checked for exit wounds and broken bones. He shook it off and ran to play. So in my opinion, his first "trail name" was Danger Nick.

Nick's determination and ingenuity never ceased to amaze us. Once, when he was probably about five years old, I went into the playroom to find a rope crudely tied to the leg of our sofa and then hanging out of the high ranch house window. He was learning how to rappel on his own.

More than once, neighbors came over to ask if we knew that Nick was on the roof, jumping onto the trampoline.

He unscrewed the register to the air duct system and climbed through the walls of the house to spy on Santa one year. We could hear him, but couldn't find him for what seemed like a long time. Ha! He definitely kept us on our toes!

Nick's pictures in the photo album used to be like looking at hidden pictures or *Where's Waldo?*, except looking for Band-Aids or bandages. There was a visible injury somewhere. ALL. THE. TIME. I got adept at removing stitches at home.

When he was in middle school, he broke both of his heels playing soccer—just a few months apart. We didn't know it at the time because he would complain that his foot hurt, but he still went hunting, still played basketball, and still played soccer. He only complained when he was supposed to load the dishwasher or go to bed. Finally, I took him to the doctor and the X-ray showed he had a fracture! I felt like a TERRIBLE mother. I cried at the doctor's office and Nick kept telling me, "Don't worry Mom. I'll be fine."

So, do I worry when he is out in the wilderness with bears, snakes, wolves, spiders, extreme weather, widowmakers, loneliness, forest fires, no GPS, no trails, poisonous plants, injuries, re-supply issues…you bet! But I also know that he has researched and prepared. He is good about keeping us posted and we follow his Garmin link to see his progress as he runs the trails. He is in better shape than before, and I don't know another single person with his mental fortitude so he's got an advantage—I hear that's the toughest part of a thru-hike. I'm not surprised that he has the itch to do the PCT. I can't wait to read about it!

And yes, his wife, Hannah, is a SAINT!

ABOUT THE AUTHOR

NICK FOWLER is an author, speaker, and long-distance hiker best known for setting the self-supported Fastest Known Time on the Pacific Crest Trail—2650 miles in 52 days, without a crew, without showers, and almost entirely fueled by junk food and bad decisions.

He's the kind of guy who'll sleep in the dirt to save $89 on a cheap motel—and then calculate the compound interest on that decision over 30 years. Former suit-and-tie guy turned hiker trash, he believes there are values to be learned from both worlds.

This book was written for anyone bold (or foolish) enough to believe that discomfort, discipline, and a dash of chaos can lead to something extraordinary.